EMPTINESS & *Brightness*

Don Cupitt

Polebridge Press

Emptiness and Brightness

Published in 2001 by Polebridge Press, P. O. Box 6144, Santa Rosa, California, 95406.

Library of Congress Cataloging-in-Publication Data

Cupitt, Don.
   Emptiness and brightness / Don Cupitt
      p. cm.
   Includes bibliographical references and index.
   ISBN 0-944344-87-9 (alk. paper)
      1. Religion--Philosophy. 2. Language and languages--Religious
aspects. I. Title.

BL51 .C835 2001
210--dc21

                                                    2001051149

Contents

Preface

For many years people have been noticing that my books and ideas tend to fall into triads. So, recently, the three studies of religious thought in everyday speech (1999/2000) have been followed by a triple testament, stating my final outlook first as *Philosophy's Own Religion* (2000), then as the kingdom theology of *Reforming Christianity* (2001), and now here as the emergent common outlook of a Second Axial Age.

The point of these three variations upon a single theme is of course to emphasize that there must be no privileged vocabulary and no such thing as a definitive statement. Each time one should make a fresh start – a principle I have always followed to the extent of not reading any of my own books! So once again I say it: a standardized technical vocabulary is very necessary in science but horrible in art, religion, and philosophy. Always start afresh. Try again.

This book is dedicated to some fellow-voyagers with whom Sea of Faith members have been meeting recently. They include the Fellows and Associates of the Westar Institute's Jesus Seminar in the USA and SnowStar in Canada. And thanks again to Linda Allen, who has remained cheerful while word-processing my last twenty-five or so books through all their many stages of revision and correction. I don't know how she does it.

I have incurred another debt while this book has been in production, to Hilary Lawson for his big book of non-realist philosophy, *Closure: a story of everything* (London and New York: Routledge 2001), which is very close to my outlook.

D.C.
Cambridge, 2001

$\mathcal{I}$ntroduction

Now teach yourself religious thinking!

Over many years, and in a long series of books, I have been trying to dismantle orthodox Latin, or 'Western', Christian theology – that is, I have been trying to reduce its iron grip on our religious imagination – in order to allow free religious thinking to be rediscovered.

The early Latin theologians were in many cases qualified lawyers, whose approach to religion was heavily influenced by legal metaphors and ways of thinking. Later, in the early medieval period, canon lawyers became dominant at Rome. They helped to institutionalise a longstanding tendency to turn faith into The Faith – controlled by lawyers and imposed upon all believers as law. Religion came to be seen as *creed*: that is, it was a matter of holding the correct doctrinal beliefs by faith and on the authority of the church. Orthodox belief was a *duty*, and deviation from it was a punishable offence. One consequence of this conception of religious faith was that there seemed to be little or no space within 'orthodoxy' for personal intellectual exploration and development: you were expected to adhere to just the same creed from the day of your admission to membership in the Church until the day of your death.

In such a setting the Church became not just a spiritual state but almost a totalitarian ideological state and an absolute monarchy, which preserved a good deal of the vocabulary and outlook of the old Christian Roman Empire. Religious life and the religious imagination were allowed to run only along theologically approved

1

channels. Religious writing was instinctively read by everyone as if by an inquisitor – i.e., with a view to deciding what doctrine it taught and judging whether that doctrine was orthodox. People still do read religious writing in that way, as I have found with my books: before all else, people feel they need to know whether the author of the text they read is a friend or an enemy – one of us or one of them, sound or unsound, an insider or an outsider, someone to be praised, or someone to be condemned.

This theologically dominated approach to religion is still not dead, even though today the authority of the Church and of orthodox credal belief have declined almost to nothing. There yet remain numerous vestiges of the old assumptions, and this puts us in some difficulty. For we are now all of us aware that new religious thinking for a new era is urgently needed, but we don't know how to set about it. How do you *do* religious thinking without the Church and its belief system, without God, and without the old supernatural world? What *is* religion, in a time when everything that we were brought up to think of as defining religion has disappeared? Theology has been so dominant for so long that we no longer know what pure and free religious thinking is.

As the old landmarks fade away and the old inhibitions weaken, religious life therefore becomes more and more pluralistic and disorderly. 'Alternatives' proliferate, and charismatic control freaks rule over tiny sects. Almost all religious writing begins to sound like gobbledygook. I don't want to use the language of 'restoring order' or 'reimposing controls', but I do ask myself, and have often asked myself, how one can today write a decent religious book in clear and honest prose. We need to go back to the beginnings of our tradition and learn to rethink the old topics of the human condition and the way to happiness, without recourse to the old assumptions and vocabularies. I'm talking about a free, fresh start with a clear head.

To go back to this kind of thinking, I should add, is to go back to a time before there was any felt need to distinguish between religious thinking, philosophical thinking, and just thinking. We are trying to go back to the point at which reflective individuals first began to try to understand what the world is, what the human self is, how we are related to the world and to other selves, what we can know, and how we should live. In science a long tradition requires us to draw away from our own selves and describe features of the world as if from the point of view of a dispassionate ideal observer; but the way we are here learning to think is evidently not scientific, because the thinker's own self is very actively engaged. What am I? How do I come to be here? How should I live? What can I hope for? Scientific thinking is secondary and developed relatively later, whereas the primal religious or philosophical questioning that we are to be concerned with here starts as soon as individuals become self-conscious, look about them, and begin to feel that our life is a puzzle. Animals have in many cases very complex social lives and are much concerned to secure and hold their social place; but human beings are concerned not only with their place in human society but also with their place in a wider, cosmic context. This *cosmic* wonder seems to be distinctively human: sometimes it takes the form of wonder about beginnings and endings (where have we come from, why are we here, and where are we going?), and sometimes it takes the form of wonder about consciousness, or about morality, or about death. But whatever form it takes, it seems to be our fate to be a puzzle to ourselves and to seek a satisfactory understanding of our place and our prospects in relation to the whole scheme of things.

From what has been said you will have gathered that by 'religious thinking' I do not mean 'theology', if by that is meant the historical study and the defence of just one tradition of faith. Nor do I mean the kind of competitive debate that always goes on within every tradition that has its own distinctive vocabulary, assumptions, and methods of argument. Nor do I mean the comparative study and evaluation of the various 'world religions', carried out with the aim, perhaps, of deciding which of them is true.

No: by pure religious thinking I mean the attempt to make a fresh start. Nothing in religion can be taken for granted any longer, and it certainly cannot be assumed that one of the world religions must be the true one. It is much more likely that all of our received traditions and methods of argument are now spent. *No* major religious tradition is still in its prime and still creative. There may be a few scraps of good stuff here and there in the great religions, but for the most part their institutions, their ways of thinking, their vocabularies, and so on are out of date and just plain wrong. In short, it seems that the long period of relative stability that followed the First Axial Age (about 800–200 B.C.E.) has now ended. If so, we should already be thinking in terms of a Second Axial Age, a time of revolutionary intellectual change, in philosophy, religion and world-view. In this book I use the term 'Axial Age' for the revolutionary years when the basic paradigms are being changed and the term 'Axial Period' for the subsequent millennia of 'normal', regularly developing cultural and religious life within the new paradigms.[1]

We are talking, then, about learning how to make a completely fresh start. If another Plato or another Buddha were to appear today, what would he have to say? Imagine him taking up again the old, good questions: What is the self? What is the world? In what ways are we interwoven with each other and with our world? What is wrong with us? How can we set about changing ourselves and our world in order to attain the highest happiness or blessedness that is accessible to us?

As we have said, these questions are religious, at least in the sense that they involve the self and its place in the world, and are practical. In the First Axial Age the ordinary person seeking salvation or blessedness typically asked 'What shall I *do*?', whereas science typically requires us to set aside the self and its concerns and to look at phenomena from the standpoint of a detached observer. However, it is obvious that the huge development of knowledge in the modern period is the main factor that has changed the human situation and so has ended the First Axial Period and opened a Second Axial Age. We have to learn to rethink all the basic assumptions, not only because the self, the world, and the relations between them are now very different, but also because *knowledge* has changed so much.

Here is an example. The First Axial Age was an Age of great founding teachers, gurus, geniuses, masters. But science tends to democratize knowledge. Individual subjectivity is left out: in principle, theories are and have to be testable by anyone who knows how to apply the appropriate test procedures. In this present book I am saying that in the Second Axial Age religion will outgrow the old teacher/disciple relationship and will become democratized. There are already no more geniuses. Truth is an emergent, continually shifting consensus, and everybody has in principle equal access to it and a contribution to make. That's the situation that our late modern information technologies are creating. So in this book my concern is *not* to impose my system upon you, but rather to show you an already emergent new philosophy, ethic, and world-picture, and to show you what religious thinking is and how you can get involved with it and play your own full part. I'm seeking to democratize pure religious thinking. This has never been done before – unless, perhaps, by the Quakers? – but I'm trying to do it now.

Here are four recommendations to get you started. *First*, we should concentrate on the old, simple questions, thinking about language, thinking about consciousness, thinking about the world and the self, thinking about Be-ing (as I call it), and thinking about happiness. It is best to simplify as much as possible and to learn to stay with a topic. Keep it in mind, or at the back of your mind, overnight or for days at a time. Let it tick over inside you.

Second, think of yourself as trying to find out what you yourself really think. Put aside all borrowed ideas and try to deliver yourself of what you have inside yourself. Be your own midwife. Listen to your own gut instincts, and listen to language as it runs spontaneously inside your head while you are drifting in the twilit world between waking and sleeping. As you will see in what follows, where language stirs inside the self, the power of world making stirs within each human person. Everything flows out of us; we have gradually generated and differentiated our whole world from within and have stabilized it by conversing with each other. It follows that pure religious thinking is a return into a primal creativity of which we all have something within ourselves.

Third, be guided by your hates as well as your loves. I have myself several times received a decisive stimulus by reading a book that provoked me to say: 'Whatever I think, I do at least know that it is *not that!*' By thinking and writing *against* ideas that we instinctively reject, we can help ourselves to develop our own thinking and to discover what we really love. I make this point because creative religious thinking has so far been very rare and very difficult, so that in order to learn it you are going to have to become an unscrupulous magpie, stealing ideas from others and learning some curious tricks in order to coax new ideas out of yourself.

And *fourth*, and finally, don't forget that it is necessary to pass through a stage of complete loss, or nihilism, in order to reach the new world and way of thinking. By nihilism I mean the questioning and the loss of all the deep philosophical assumptions that have underpinned Western culture since Plato. People who try to think out a new position without first clearing their heads merely repeat all the errors of the past: hence the plethora of muddled New Age movements, alternative cults, and complementary therapies that infest our contemporary world. Have nothing to do with any of them. Instead, follow the Purgative Way and go for nihilism. No cross, no crown, as believers used to say.

Chapter One

Beginning Again

The new Axial Age

Karen Armstrong has recently been suggesting[*] that we are living in a second Axial Age. The first Axial Age – a phrase taken from Karl Jaspers – lasted from about 800 to 200 years B.C.E. It was the period when across the Old World, in China, India, and Greece, the first great individual thinkers – people like Plato and the Buddha – were busy inventing philosophy and laying down standard conceptions of the world, the self, knowledge, action, the good life, and so on. Around these ideas whole cultural traditions, and indeed great religions, were to develop in the course of time. For example, classical Christianity both Catholic and Orthodox has always been heavily indebted to Plato's ideas about the soul and the body, about the changing visible world below and the eternal world above, and about human life as a journey through time to our last home in the eternal world. There is much justice in Nietzsche's description of Catholicism as 'platonism for the masses'.

The great Axial Age thinkers created at least three major cultural traditions, those of the West, India, and China, that each lasted for at least 2000 years; but now the huge knowledge explosion that began in the West with the Revival of Learning and the take-off of early modern science is coming to look like the single greatest event in the

* In a paper so far unpublished that was presented to the Spring Conference 2001 of the Westar Institute at Rohnert Park, California. But Karen Armstrong went on to argue that we have not yet fully understood the radicalism of the great teachers of the First Axial Age, so that she probably does not go as far as I do in wanting to try for a fresh start.

whole of known human history. (I say 'known', because we can't date its rival, the origin of language.) This great truth-event, which we may see as beginning with the work of Erasmus and Copernicus, has changed everything, and has now — so Karen Armstrong is suggesting — opened a second Axial Age, an epoch in which we must be prepared to rethink everything. We need to be talking about a radically fresh start: we need to be as uncompromisingly bold in our day as the great founders of our religious and philosophical traditions were in theirs.

Some people will object that this line of argument is much less relevant to Buddhism and to China than it is to Christianity. Thus the principal Buddhist philosopher, Nagarjuna, who perhaps belongs to the second or third century of the Common Era, still stands up remarkably well and is far superior to equivalent figures in other traditions. Intellectually, Buddhism is in better shape than the other principal faiths. And it may also be argued that we are not yet in any position to say that China's ancient cultural traditions in ethics and religion have been finally lost. Christianity is not so well placed, for it is undeniably true that classical Christian thought was always heavily dependent upon platonism. But it now appears that the revolution in philosophy that came about with the work of Kant and Hegel marked the end of the old régime: it has turned out to be the end of platonism, the end of metaphysics, and the Death of God all at once. Popular Christian language in the nineteenth century remained steeped in platonism, but, as we sense in Victorian hymnody, the old platonic yearning for heaven is turning unawares into an intense nostalgia for a platonism that is inexorably slipping away. Without really knowing it, Victorian piety was a long sad farewell. Then in the twentieth century everyone became aware that platonic realism and the platonic distinctions between appearance and reality, body and soul, and time and eternity were suddenly gone. Plato was dead — and the Christian tradition began to collapse. Thus it seems undeniable that in the Christian world at least, radical innovation is needed and has begun; but it may yet be claimed that so far as Buddhism and China are concerned the jury is still out.

Maybe: but one suspects that the current globalization of economic and cultural life is having much the same effect upon traditional culture everywhere. Everywhere it secularizes and 'detraditionalizes' people; everywhere it makes the past seem irrelevant.

Everywhere it has already created a spiritual crisis, and we have to be ready to think previously unheard of thoughts.

Pure religious thinking

If all our received religious traditions have now come to an end and a Second Axial Age has perhaps already begun, then we need radically new religious thinking. We need, for a time at least, to abandon the old institutions, the old doctrines, the old vocabularies, and even the old assumptions about what religion is. Thus 'pure' religious thinking is a post-traditional kind of thinking that breaks with the past and attempts to make a new beginning.

For example, most faiths and most thinkers of the First Axial Age were characterized by a certain *spiritual individualism*. It was accepted that the religiously serious individual should give priority to the pursuit of personal salvation. Furthermore, First Axial philosophies and faiths often believed that we should orient our lives towards a Reality or a Real World out there. The Real was not identified with the apparent world of everyday life, which was usually seen as being very unsatisfactory. Rather, the Real was an eternal, intelligible Being or Order which lay beyond the apparent world and somehow upheld it. So we should seek individual salvation, we should seek it beyond the apparent world, and we would find it by gaining access to or union with a blessed, time transcending Reality.

All these ideas must now be abandoned. They are wrong and badly out of date. We differ from the great figures of the First Axial Age in that our world is now almost completely theorized by science and has thereby become appropriated to us. Secondly, we have become acutely aware of language, and in particular of the way our language runs everywhere, forming and shaping both ourselves and our world. The result of these two great truth events combined has been the end of metaphysics, the end of 'mystery', and the end of belief in a more Real world beyond the apparent world. There is no ready-made Real World out there, and there is no ready-made real self.

We don't need metaphysics. Look around you: what you see is only sense experience which has been formed as such by our language, and by language (including the language of our theory) has been stitched together to make a continuous world. *We* assemble it all, and *we* give to it its apparent 'reality'. The last relic of metaphysics is simply everything's Be-ing in time: that is, the gentle, constant forthcoming of everything as it gives itself to us. But Be-ing is extra-linguistic: that is, it is only that which gives itself to and emerges clothed in language, and it is not anything that can be pinned down and interrogated by language. Be-ing is only the way everything comes . . . to pass, in time. It is universal contingency, the passing show. It is all there is, and it is not mysterious or deep in any way at all. It is simply the contingent existing of things in time. It includes us, and we too are constructs, part of it all.

This new way of seeing the human condition is radically 'immanentist' or naturalistic. There is only one world, and it is this one; and we human beings have only one home, and it is in this world. It follows that the new 'pure' religious thinking of the Second Axial Period will be markedly different from the older type of religious thought. We are indeed still concerned about the self, the world, and the relation between them, and we are still concerned to find and follow the way to lasting happiness. But we don't believe in any soul or core self, and we don't orient ourselves towards a more Real person or order that supposedly transcends the apparent world. On the contrary, there is only 'Becoming', the flux of things, and only the apparent world. But we are not anxious about transience, and we do not complain that there is something radically unsatisfactory about this world of ours. On the contrary, Second Axial Age thinking rejects the old appearance-reality distinction. The world is *our* world, and our world is the only world. The self and its world produce each other and belong entirely to each other. Thus we find our complete religious happiness in the love of life, now. We commit ourselves entirely and exclusively to our own world and to our transient lives, and that's *it*. There is nothing else.

Notice the extent to which religion has changed and the extent to which it has *not* changed. Religion hasn't changed insofar as it is still concerned with coming to a correct understanding of our human condition, and it is still about the path and the practices by which we can attain a reliable kind of happiness. But religion *has* changed in that the way to eternal happiness is now by saying an unqualified Yes to our transient life in this world of ours. We are not a bit interested in saving our souls by keeping them unspotted from the world; instead, we are ecstatically happy to pour ourselves out and pass away.

Immediate religion

By 'immediate' religion, I don't mean religion without delay: I mean religion that is not mediated. In the First Axial Period most religions became approximately platonic in shape, in the sense that the believer aspired after something supremely and eternally Real that lay beyond the world of sense. It was beyond the range not only of his senses, but also of his understanding: he could not see it or even think it but somehow he knew that he was made for it and meant for it. His relation to it could not be direct but had to be *mediated* by symbols or icons. These symbolic mediators were of many kinds, and when taken all together they made up a very large and complex apparatus: the Scriptures, the church, the priesthood, rituals, myths, works of art, festivals, systems of doctrine, and so forth. The whole system of mediation was sanctified by tradition, was often spoken of as a Way or Path, and took a distinctive form in each major faith community.

From this account it will be evident why, in the historical period just ending, we tended simply to equate 'a religion' with 'a particular apparatus of religious mediation, considered as a systematic whole'. It will also be evident why for the past two and a bit millennia the besetting sin of all religious people has been *a certain fetishism of the apparatus*. This happens because the apparatus tends to get sanctified by tradition and to be sanctified also by its association with the god or the blessedness towards which it is thought to be leading the faithful. Inevitably, people everywhere have concluded that the apparatus is sacrosanct: it cannot be altered in any detail, so that we can take a great pride in it, brandish it as a badge of difference, and demand unswerving loyalty to it. Thus in the historical epoch just ended, or ending, the means always tended to become an end in itself, and there was a very close relationship between faith and ethnic allegiance. First Axial religion easily degenerated into superstition or into a religious version of nationalism.

In the Second Axial Period, however, there is no more real order beyond the present world, and religion becomes immediate and objectless. It becomes a matter of the way we commit ourselves, existentially and ethically, simply to life in the here and now. The scale of the change is roughly indicated by a comparison between the Roman Catholic Church, the biggest and grandest example of the mediated type of religion, and the Society of Friends, one of the best examples extant of the immediate sort of religion in which the vast symbolic apparatus of mediation has simply dropped away. Take that contrast, and magnify it somewhat (because even Quakers still have some belief in God and some attachment to forms) and you have some indication of the scale of the change that is coming.

Notice that immediate religion is beliefless and autonomous. It is an overflowing joy. The notion of the *autonomy* of religion needs a little further comment, because in the past we have been accustomed to the idea that a great pre-established Metaphysical Fact claims us and prescribes its orientation to our religious life. That is realism: religion is seen as a *response* to something more Real that precedes us in every way. But through Kant and Nietzsche we gradually got used to the idea of the autonomy of ethics, coming to see that there is no morality out there, that morality is wholly human, and that we must joyfully posit and love our values purely for their own sakes. *The autonomy of religion* extends the same principles to religion. There is no pre-existent Reality out there. There is only Be-ing, and Be-ing is pretty much the same thing as what physicists call 'quantum fluctuations in the vacuum' – i.e., a dance of possibility in the Void. That's all there is out there. So I increasingly see the future as 'nihilism' – and I mean a nihilism that has become joyful, affirmative, and active: a nihilism that will in time seem to itself to be perfectly ordinary and easy. And against this background we acknowledge that religion is wholly human and that we must posit our religious values and attitudes purely for their own sakes. The *autonomy of religion* means *spontaneous* religiousness, religion without bondage and without guilt: religion whose actual, joyous practice is its only reward.

I am making religion seem so short-term, intense, and momentary that you are going to wonder what religious *thinking* can be on this view of religion and what *spirituality* is. The word 'spirituality' is unfortunate, because it gets such force as it still has from an implied contrast between things spiritual and things temporal. But I am insisting that everything is temporal and there is nothing that is non-temporal; so what is left for 'spirituality' to be?

In reply, we simply refuse the spiritual-temporal distinction, with its picture of the human being as simultaneously living two different lives in two distinct worlds – a natural human life with others in time and a spiritual life in which we relate ourselves continually to God in eternity. On the contrary, there is only one world for us, and we live only one life. This transient life is *itself* our 'spiritual' life. As for religious thinking, it engages the human condition as we are now coming to understand it and turns it into lyric poetry – poetry about Be-ing, and about the ways in which our life is interwoven with our world, and interwoven also with other lives. We think about the way language spills out of the self and is poured over the whole field of experience, shaping things, building the world, and developing our relationships with other people; and as we think of these things, they turn into poetry in our heads.[1]

The end of the Real

We need to think more about just what we lost when we lost the old belief in the Cosmos as a ready-made and objective Real World, out there and laid on just for us. How much did we lose, and how do we manage without it: what will take its place?

One thing that takes its place is the history of science. The old Cosmos was a divinely instituted world order, a fixed stage for human life that was going to remain in place unchanged from the day when God rested after completing his work of Creation, all the way through until Judgement Day. Instead of this traditional picture of a fixed divine order, we now have a history of human world pictures, from the very first unified cosmos in Upper Palaeolithic times (around 12,000 years ago, that is) all the way through to the exotic speculations of today's physical cosmologists. Notice that as science gets ever bigger and grander, theory changes faster, and the world gets fainter. Today it is not so much a world as a whirl of rapidly changing and very fanciful cosmological theories.

So the world is our own fast evolving picture of the world, and we cannot distinguish between the two. We never see the world absolutely: we see only the world of our current theory; and because we see only the world of our current theory, the world in each successive generation always seems obligingly to be giving empirical confirmation to our current theory! That's fine; but we have no way of thinking about a real world out there, fixed and independent of our theory.

Let's spell this out: the world of your present experience – the world about you just at this moment – consists of a crackle and a prickle of points of sensation, tingles in your sensory nerves which have been formed into sensory *qualia* (greens, sweetnesses, rumbles, and the like) by language, and by language again have been stitched together and assembled into a continuous world about you. Furthermore, the motion of language inside your head doesn't just build you a continuous and theorized ambient world: it also makes the world *bright*. That is, it makes your experience of the world *conscious*. Remember the biblical myth: *Light* was the very first thing that language made! It is this light – the brightness of the world, the consciousness of conscious experience – which is the most religiously primal and wonderful thing there is. It dazzles me every day. Open your eyes to it.

With the gradual development during the twentieth century of this new world picture came by degrees the end of the Real – the end of the notion that something out there independently validates our knowledge and determines the way things are. On the contrary, as we now see it, we have to forget all forms of the notion that something supremely Real out there controls reality and grounds all of our knowledge and values. On the contrary, what we see as being out there is only our own ever changing projection. There is no objective reality, no objective truth, no objective value, and no objective or absolute knowledge. It sounds terrifying, and you may wonder why I should wish to say such things; but there is no way through to the new experience of religious joy that I am talking about, except by going through this moment of nihilism. I want more than a temporary suspension of your disbelief: I want you to turn around completely and learn to practise a new world view.

Forgetting about the Real, the Old Out-There, enables us to receive a new way of seeing the world in which ontology is replaced by semeiosis. That is, we renounce old thinking about being and real existence, and we replace it with the new time conditioned thinking about the gentle forthcoming process of Be-ing and the process of linguistic Mean-ing, 'semeiosis', that forms everything. We've got to learn to think — and again I suggest that we do it best when we are lying relaxed in bed — in the new gentle, contingent, 'process' mode about the way Be-ing gives itself, always in time, and about the way the movement of language shapes or in-forms everything, again, always within the flow of time. Learn to think *slowly*, and above all, lightly.

Chapter Two

Hard Labour?

So just how difficult is all this necessary rethinking going to be? Very difficult indeed, you might well think, for religious institutions have taken pains to protect themselves by teaching that religious truth is rare and precious. It is much too exalted for any solitary individual to be capable of discovering it unaided. It must be communicated to us by a divine revelation, which is guarded by an exclusive, divinely commissioned institution whose interpretation of it is definitive. The individual who attempts to criticize and change church teaching is thus beating his head against a brick wall. A personally elected point of view is a 'heresy', from the Greek verb *haireomai*, choose; and (as everyone knows) heretics are wrong by definition.

Official doctrine, then, teaches that the individual hasn't a chance. Historically, he got burnt. After the Enlightenment, he was no longer subject to the old physical punishments, but he has continued to be given a bad time, as a very long line of great names can bear witness. Even today, the theologian who is perceived to be a transgressor is still punished. Gerd Lüdemann of the University of Göttingen suffers as I write.*

---

* Lüdemann, originally a Lutheran, is being punished very much as the Catholic Hans Küng was punished twenty years ago – by being prevented from teaching students for the professional ministry.

There is more: those whose thinking leads them to question and perhaps to reject the deep assumptions of the tradition in which they were brought up risk very severe inner conflict and even self-punishment. Charles Darwin in his rooms in London in the late 1840s is a familiar example. He was working out the details of his great theory even as the Chartists marched in the streets outside his window. Darwin was raised in the old Establishment, in a 'county' family and in the Church of England, at Shrewsbury School under Dr. Butler and at Christ's College, Cambridge, in the old Christian platonism and the Argument from Design. But now the development of his own thinking was aligning him with new social and cultural forces abroad in society that would in time destroy the cultural world that was his own homeland. The resulting psychological conflict partly disabled him. He remained a good husband and father and a faithful friend, and he successfully completed his life's work. But he had to live quietly and avoid public exposure.

The punishment in such a case is inflicted by one's own psychology. Thus, a theologian who has to do a good deal of public speaking and lecturing, and whose thinking is leading him more and more to question the tradition for which he is perceived to be a spokesman, may actually silence himself as tension in his larynx makes him unable to speak. When this happened to me in 1991, I soon began to hear of many others who had been or were still in the same predicament and found that they have included some very well-known names. I understood why some of the heretics of old had gone gladly to the stake. Emotionally, they agreed with their persecutors and welcomed the flames.

The most extreme and exalted case is of course that of Friedrich Nietzsche, the most gifted individual of modern times, whose critique and rejection of the values and assumptions of his own tradition was exceptionally thoroughgoing. He drove himself to a higher level of anxiety and a more spectacular collapse than anyone else has achieved or suffered. *That* is the price you must be ready to pay, if you think it is your duty to criticize and rethink your own tradition.

This prompts the question: Why has our cultural and religious tradition been imprinted upon us with such terrifying violence that we cannot escape from it without risking psychological ruin? I think I can understand why David Hume had to have a breakdown in order to get out of Calvinism and why today so many people still need a breakdown in order to get out of Evangelicalism. *But why is metaphysical realism just as terrifyingly violent and hard to escape?*

Here I will reply only briefly to this question. A realist is a person who believes in the objectivity of knowledge, who believes in a ready-made, ordered and intelligible world – a *cosmos* – out there, someone who believes in truth-out-there and meaning-out-there. A scientific realist is a person who believes that what's in the current textbook of physics somehow copies the shape of what's out there. Don't ask too persistently exactly what this copying relation consists in, because it is impossible to say clearly, but the scientific realist is a person who believes, to speak poetically, that 'God is a scientist'; for to believe that the laws of nature somehow exist out there, and that Truth is out there, is at least half way to believing in a great cosmic *Mind* out there that thinks and wills the world order.

None of this can be right, not least because it is always the case that more than one theory will 'save the phenomena', and we can never know for sure that present theory is final and built-in. How could we know such a thing? But it is what many scientists need to believe, and therefore *do* half believe. God is a scientist, and the human scientist whose mind is made in the image of God thinks God's thoughts after him. Scientific theories, these scientists believe, are not invented but discovered, and scientific discoveries involve an illumination of the human mind by God. The scientist's contemplation of Nature is a sort of worship.

There is still a link, I am saying, between realism and theism, and that perhaps is why many people in the West cling tenaciously to realism despite the fact that we live two hundred years after Kant and Hegel's revolution in philosophy. Scientific realism is a substitute for the old religion, and it isn't true; but it remains very tempting, and it can be very dogmatic.

Chapter Three

Solitary Buddhas

I have been saying that the kind of rethinking we now have to attempt is likely to be extremely difficult and stressful, for we are struggling to free ourselves from habits of thinking that were impressed upon us long ago and with great violence. Religious truth, we are told, is inaccessible to unaided human reason. It has been supernaturally communicated to humans. A great institution guards it and controls its interpretation. Furthermore, this great institution has impeccable historical credentials: it has always taught exactly the same saving truth, transmitted unchanged down an unbroken line of properly accredited teachers ever since the very beginning.

You have been warned: your chances of doing better than the Church and finding the truth on your own are nil. Yet religious thought is so dialectical that you can always find the opposite being said somewhere, and there is a strong contrary tradition insisting that religious truth is obvious. It is so close to us that we fail to notice it. It is right under our noses. We need only to wake up to it. The talented (if eccentric) theological writer Austen Farrer once defined the task of apologetics as 'the defence of platitudes against sophistries', and one knows what he means.

Nagarjuna made the point within the Buddhist tradition by coining the term *pratyeka-buddha*, 'solitary Buddhas', to describe people who discover Enlightenment independently, through their own insight into contingency and universal Emptiness:

> When buddhas don't appear
> And their followers are gone,
> The wisdom of awakening
> Bursts forth by itself.[1]

Or, as Garfield translates the last two lines: 'The wisdom of the self-enlightened ones/Will arise completely without a teacher'.[2] When we first study Nagarjuna himself, he seems astonishingly radical and even nihilistic. It is difficult to grasp such an uncompromising thinker. But from another point of view all he is doing is simply stating the obvious – spelling out clearly and consistently what is implied by the recognition that everything in our experience, and everything within ourselves too, is contingent and changing. And similarly, Buddhists normally insist upon the importance of lengthy training under the guidance of a recognized teacher from a strong teaching lineage; but Nagarjuna is saying that the central Buddhist insight is not far from Nietzsche's idea of 'the innocence of becoming'. Completely to accept universal contingency and transience, within and without, is bliss – and this thought is so easy to come at that it may occur to anyone at any time. Institutional Buddhism, with its emphasis on loyalty to the sangha and obedience to an authoritative teacher from a sound lineage, worries about the successful transmission of the truth unchanged through time. But even if institutional Buddhism were to vanish altogether, Enlightenment is so easy and obvious that it may pop up again anywhere and at any time. Tradition is not the only way to truth, and religious truth is not always hard to grasp. It can be blindingly easy.

So it can often come about that after decades of spiritual struggle a person comes to a position and a point of view in which he or she is able to rest – and then finds someone else there already, who says: 'This is where I have always been, this is what I've always thought: it seems obvious to me'. The same idea or 'position' that to one person is very hard won, to another person may be easy and even platitudinous.

How can this be? It comes about because our minds don't start off as blank slates. We live within language, and a great deal of the history of ideas underlies the way language habitually runs inside us. My 'mind' is a large and miscellaneous collection of mostly bad linguistic habits left over from the philosophy and the religion of the past, and many of them can be shaken off only with very great difficulty. In order to do any kind of new thinking in philosophy, in religion, and in ethics we all of us need to begin with our personal programme of unlearning. We need *anti*-philosophy, *anti*-religion, and even *anti*-ethics in order to clear our heads. Of course we differ greatly amongst ourselves in just what we need most to unlearn, but that is why it can come about that one person may have to go through years of painful unlearning before she can reach a position that (irritatingly) turns out to be another person's easy and obvious starting-point.*

Religious truth is easy and obvious and is this: To say a whole-hearted Yes to life in full acknowledgement of its gratuitousness, its contingency, its transience, and even its nothingness– is bliss. What is interesting to each person is the angle by which she has come to this realization, her personal journey, the route she's taken. But if so, it may very well be the case that the elementary insights that I've cudgelled my brains for forty-five years to reach have always seemed to you to be utterly obvious. You don't need this book. It's too platitudinous.

---

*The greatest and commonest mistake in religious thought is that made by the millions of people who today embrace 'spirituality' and New Age thinking without first clearing their heads. They rush uncritically into an untidy jumble of ideas: they have not sufficiently purged themselves of platonism and so forth, and therefore, instead of escaping from the errors of the past, they merely repeat them. We need to train ourselves to be thoroughly sceptical and emptied out before we can learn to think more clearly. See also ch. 18.

Chapter Four

Humanism after the Turn to Language

In religion the same proposition may be to one person a platitude and to another a bombshell.

For example, suppose that we have counted the cost and are willing to pay the price. Suppose that we do embark upon a sustained critique and deconstruction of the religious tradition that we have inherited, and suppose also that we immerse ourselves in the best contemporary art and philosophy. Over the years we are led gradually to acknowledge that the basic truth from which everything should start is the truth of 'naturalism' (as the Anglo-Saxons call it; on the Continent the term 'materialism' is usually preferred).

Let's spell this out: Everything is contingent, everything is transient, everything is 'Empty' (in the Buddhist sense: it lacks a stable, permanent essence of its own. It consists merely in its own shifting relations with everything else). Everything is a product of time and chance. We should see the world – that is, we should see all reality – as a fountain, a silent ceaseless outpouring of purely contingent Being, which all the time is getting coded into signs in our seeing of it and then passes away, perhaps to be recycled. The world is a flux of happenstance. Everything just happens, everything is just hap, and of course all this is as true also of ourselves, our ideas, our words, our values, our thoughts and fears, as it is of the so-called external world. Notice that *philosophically* there is no difference between *our* world and *the* world, for such intelligibility and order as the world has it gets through us, in our seeing of it. In us the empty flux of be-ing gets coded into signs, because we see everything in terms of words and numbers and thereby make it all into a brightly lit, consciously seen and possessed world of our own. Only through us does the world become world. Thus the human art vision of the world is all the world we have, and lovely in its beauty, transience and nihility. Everything is Empty, you are Empty too, and (as the Christian apostle says) all things are yours.

That, very sketchily, is Empty radical humanism. The communally evolved human lifeworld, that is, the world of our human 'life', is endless and outsideless like the world of a soap opera – soaps being a philosophically very instructive postmodern art form: they are nihilistic, they are Empty, they don't ever really start or finish, they are endless, they are humanistic, they just go on, and they are utterly absorbing. People like soaps so much that (so one gathers) most people in the modern West live in and follow more than one of them; and in any case, is not our contemporary celebrity culture simply society itself seen as a great soap opera?

Empty radical humanism started with people like Charles Dickens and by now is normality. It is for most people the obvious truth of life that they have taken for granted for over a century. It is banal, it is ordinariness. Life's a novel, life's a baggy shapeless holdall, life is all there is. And yet if I spell it out philosophically in post-Derridean, post-Ecoic, and post-Baudrillardian language, it may sound terrifyingly strange and nihilistic; and I myself may be filled with metaphysical horror at the collapse of the old notion of the objectively real. When explained, Empty radical humanism can also sound pseudish, and may attract the sarcasm of one or another of the snobbish Enlightenment conservatives who are still numerically predominant amongst us. But more often, as I sit looking out of the window and thinking, Empty radical humanism fills me with indestructible joy. I am an unusually visual person who is often ravished by the visual field. So I gaze at the view – and this passing show, this brightness, is all there is. Nothing other than it passes judgement upon it: nothing does or can devalue it. It is itself only now, in me and for me, all this; and, Empty as it is and I am, it is enough. I don't want anything to be in any way different. I am happy to pass out into all this.

Such is the new religious vision, and for an art image of it one may try New York abstract expressionist painting of the period 1940-1970: late Monet, Pollock, Newman, Rothko, Reinhardt, Still, and others too. One can see why it may seem to some terrifyingly nihilistic and to others banal. Its cutting edge is its complete acceptance of naturalism, a point which calls for further comment.

In the later Middle Ages in the West there were in the towns many worthy people — married people, burgesses, merchants, tradespeople, pillars of the community — who wanted to live a religious life. Unfortunately, the Church in those days taught a very dualistic doctrine which drew a sharp contrast between the religious life and life in the world. The best life was 'the religious life', which was a secluded contemplative celibate life, lived in community and under vows of obedience. All that the Church seemed able to offer the merchant and his wife was membership of a Third Order, as a secular tertiary. Such a person was allowed to follow a specially devised reduced version of the religious life, while still living in the world. She was a sort of honorary nun, a nun at one remove. This I think was the origin of the idea that one's religious life is a second, imaginary, 'inner' life that one lives in parallel with one's outer life in the world — an idea that the Protestant Reformation both rebelled against and perpetuated, so that it remains prominent even as late as the younger Kierkegaard, who still sees faith and religious commitment as an extra, unseen realm in which a person's inner reality is quite different from the appearance he presents to the world. And in today's barely comprehensible burbling about 'spirituality' and a 'spiritual dimension' the same old dualistic contrasts between appearance and reality, outer and inner, and the material and the spiritual are still being drawn. But it always sounds like self-indulgent nonsense nowadays.

I have been arguing that modern philosophy since Kant and Hegel has been struggling to get away from all those cliché contrasts. And amongst theologians today it would be widely agreed, I am sure, that something had gone terribly wrong in Christianity when a devout fifteenth-century townsperson was told that if she wished to progress in the religious life the way she must do it was to become an imaginary nun. The scholastic-platonic dualisms in terms of which classical Christianity was articulated are very largely to blame for Christianity's long-term decline, for it was official doctrine itself that made the religious life into a fantasy life! That was the real *trahison des clercs*.

And that, too, is why any serious attempt to criticize and rethink our tradition today will lead in the direction of naturalism. We will be struggling to free ourselves from the lingering influence of dualistic contrasts which we now see were damaging. And we see why the move to get rid of the natural/supernatural distinction and all its correlates (world/Church, body/soul, appearance/reality, sinful man/holy God, time/eternity) seems to be both obvious and platitudinous, yet daring and shocking. Because, of course, we are talking about the end of belief in God and life after death. We are talking about getting rid of the whole system of supernatural belief, and still more, about getting rid of the idea that religion involves us in feeling we are not quite all there. Why should religion involve one in being slightly abstracted all the time, secretly living out imaginary relationships with fictional beings who inhabit another world? Why should there not be religion which shows us how to recognize and respond to the truth of our life, just as it is?

That is why the religion of a new Axial Period will be immediate and beliefless. Paradoxically, it will be at once so obvious that it's very difficult to say anything at all about it, *and yet* so much literary art will be required to manoeuvre the ordinary person into seeing the obvious that it will appear sophistical and shocking.

Chapter Five

Wrestling with Life

Why do people keep diaries? Often they are adolescents, or young single women, or people who are isolated, aspiring, and preparing themselves for a future task. I am suggesting that the diary as a literary form is a way of asking the old banal question about 'the meaning of life'. The diary is a way of trying to record the ordinariness of ordinary life, a way of trying to interrogate it, to see it aright and to understand it. Thus, from my new-religion point of view, keeping a diary and trying to make sense of one's own life is a better and more non-dualistic religious practice than is 'saying one's prayers' in the traditional way.

For tragic, adventitious reasons that lie outside the text, Anne Frank's has been perhaps the best loved and most widely read of modern diaries; and perhaps what one should like most about it is not the fact that it is a work of genius but the fact that it is implicitly so democratic. Almost any young person growing up in a confined space – in a boarding school or in some isolated district – might well think just such thoughts as these and might profit by writing them down in this way. Because she is so young, it is all new and interesting to her and therefore to us. The freshness cheers up her older readers. She, at least, is not yet tired of life. She's too young as yet to have experienced eternal joy in life, but she's on the way to it.

It is sad that some people die before they have experienced eternal joy in life, but it is sadder still that so many people nowadays live long enough to become incurably tired of life and incapable of joy. The young have the advantage that while religious joy in life lies in the future, one can still have a sort of anticipatory knowledge of what it is going to be; whereas those who have become terminally tired of life are the true lost souls, for they are no longer aware that they have forgotten what joy is. That is a dreadful state for a human being to have allowed himself to get into.

Our teaching, then, is that life is all there is. Life has no outside. This inconclusive banality, this ordinariness, is *it*. And we have to make religious happiness out of it. True religion is the practice of making eternal happiness out of the flux of ordinariness by the way we attend to it, cast ourselves into it, identify ourselves with it, and relate ourselves to others in it. True religion is saying Yes to life, Yes to transience, and a wholehearted Yes to Empty radical humanism.

In platonism one holds oneself back a little from life, in the belief that the true home of our noblest part lies in a Better World elsewhere. I'm saying, on the contrary, that all this is ours, and we belong wholly to all this. Being Empty ourselves, we should identify ourselves unreservedly with the Empty flux of existence – and here we differ a little from Buddhism, for I am saying that we should not merely seek mental liberation by meditating upon Emptiness; we should actively *live* Emptiness *as freedom*. What is Empty does not have a fixed nature but consists merely of its own relations to everything else, and it can therefore be *changed* by describing it differently and by treating it differently.

And all this, I've been saying, is easy and obvious, so much so that there isn't and there doesn't need to be any specially privileged vocabulary for saying it. I have tried to make this point by varying my own vocabulary and so describing our self-identification with the Empty flux in different writings as *glory*, as *ecstatic immanence*, as *the mysticism of secondariness*, and as *solar living*. By varying the language I am trying to prevent my own teaching from being read dogmatically and being systematized. If I were so read, I would find myself being made into an enemy of the very freedom that I love most of all.

In Second Axial Period religion, we don't *need* any institutional authority, or any doctrine systems, or big hats, or religious law. We need only humble teachers, poets of truth, and tellers of stories. In the first Axial Period ideas were traced back to great charismatic founding Teachers, and indeed, belief in the supreme cultural and religious significance of the genius has in one form or another characterized the past two-and-a-half millennia. But now it's out of date. From now on there will not be any more founding geniuses of the old kind, and great shifts in thinking will take place democratically, manifesting themselves as changes in the way we speak. Thus I have tried to show that the new religion of Life is already worked out in more detail in the idioms of ordinary language than it is in the writings of people who belonged to the last generations of genius such as Nietzsche, Schweitzer, and D.H. Lawrence.[1] Ordinary language has proved itself brighter even than these great names – and this is historically a quite new and astonishing fact.

But it is true: in ordinary language life has in effect already become the new religious object, and the new religion is the practice of wrestling with life, struggling to come to terms with it, saying Yes to it, and learning how to live it to the full. The aim is to become able in the end to say Amen to one's own life.

Chapter Six

Theory and Practice

Even someone who cordially disapproves of system-building may still struggle to arrive at a coherent 'approach' and 'point of view' – feeble though those metaphors are.

So in the mid-90s I summarized my overall 'position' (another feeble metaphor) by the formula: 'Energetic Spinozism, poetical theology, solar ethics'.

By speaking of *Spinozism* I was aligning myself with the thought of Baruch Spinoza (1632–1677), the first secular Jew, and a religious naturalist who cast his thought in purely this-worldly terms. But where Spinoza used the vocabulary of metaphysical rationalism and talked of substance and necessity, I am more of a nominalist who sees the world as being something like a slow motion explosion and thinks in terms of scattering energies, motion, and contingency. In this connection I might have dug up the name of Hobbes and have associated myself with that somewhat neglected and misunderstood philosopher. But I preferred Spinoza and adopted the phrase *Energetic Spinozism*.

By *poetical theology* I signified that at that stage I was still keen to save something of Christian ecclesiastical doctrine. It might be retained, if it were understood as giving us myths and imagery to live by. By using the word *poetical* I was reminding the reader that the whole cycle of Christian myths presents us with a large body of traditional stories that can be imaginatively retold in many ways for many purposes. It is up to us to make something new out of it all.

However, a doubt arises at this point: the Christian cycle of stories is nowadays about as well-known to the general public as is the traditional 'matter of Britain', the Arthuriad, or perhaps the collection of popular ballads about Robin Hood. None of these three bodies of traditional stories is much in vogue just now, and the number of writers who can usefully be kept employed in retelling them is clearly very limited. Can anyone claim that the body of Christian stories, from Genesis to Judgement Day, still has any more moral and religious mileage in it than the Arthuriad? Does the old way of seeing all of cosmic history as the working out of a mighty drama of Fall and Redemption still grip us at all? I fear that it does not. It may be culturally valuable to be able to decipher the world view that is built into our medieval cathedrals, but it no longer makes a practical difference to the way anyone conducts her life.

Thirdly and finally, by *solar ethics* I meant a burning commitment to life seen as outpouring continuous process. We are part of the whole, and with it we pour ourselves out and we pass away:

> We should live as the Sun does. The process by which it lives and the process by which it dies are one and the same. It hasn't a care. It simply expends itself gloriously, and in so doing gives life to us all.[1]

The image came to me from various literary sources, no doubt — a few lines in Spinoza, a novel by Anthony Burgess, a libretto by W.S. Gilbert, Georges Bataille — but above all it comes from personal experience at a time of severe illness. I liked it because it met my desire for an objective, expressivist approach to ethics. I wanted to forget all about moralities driven by some inner burden of sin, karma, guilt, shame, and the fear of death. I wanted to forget inwardness, and I borrowed from Vivekananda the idea that one does not *need* to live a burden-driven life. The burden should simply be dropped. We should live like the Sun, which is nothing but its own pouring out into expression and passing away. Whereas much of classical Christian spirituality was a practice of careful self-examination and preparation for death, solar ethics lives the unity of living and dying all the time, and never needs to think about death as a distinct topic. It simply gives itself heedlessly into life and away.

Energetic Spinozism, poetical theology, and solar ethics was the formula I quoted around 1992/96. Today it has been replaced by a five point summary, as follows: universal contingency, Empty radical humanism, attention to Be-ing, solar living, and humanitarian ethics. I've introduced most of these terms already. Now we will pay them closer attention.

Chapter Seven

The New World View

Universal contingency

The doctrine of universal contingency is the doctrine that the way things go is neither meant nor fated: it all just happens, and might have happened otherwise. Happening is changing, coming to pass, or befalling. Many things happen regularly, of course; but in that case they just *happen* to happen regularly. The regularities do not *have* to be the way they are. That having been said, most philosophies other than dogmatic rationalism are happy to accept the idea of the contingency of all true empirical propositions and therefore the contingency of the world as a whole. But philosophies differ greatly in the way they interpret the idea, and some take it much further than others. For example, are you willing to accept that the moral values and principles that mean most to you are merely contingent products of history that might have evolved very differently? Are you willing to accept that your own religious faith is only a contingent product of history, a complex of ideas and values and practices that happened to come into being and in due course will no doubt happen to pass away? Are you willing to accept that our whole picture of the world and our scientific theory did not *have* to develop the way it has done and might have taken a very different form, which we might nevertheless have still been able to put to good practical use? Are you willing to accept that there are no 'absolutes' out there and nothing that compels us to impose just one pattern upon the Empty flux of things, and no other?

In brief, the most thoroughgoing interpretations of the theme of

37

universal contingency may lead one in the direction not just of prag-
matism, but also of phenomenalism, relativism, and even nihilism,
the Buddhist sublime. But at the opposite extreme a conservative
metaphysical philosopher such as Thomas Aquinas is also happy to
cite the acknowledged contingency of the world as a premise on
which to build an argument for the existence of God.

Philosophers ranging from Aquinas to Nagarjuna have, then,
been agreed that in some sense everything is contingent. Here I am
going to argue that the mainstream Western tradition has always carried along inside itself the more radical, Buddhist notion of universal
contingency. When a philosopher like Aquinas sets out to argue his
way from the world to God, he has to start off by conjuring up a picture of the world considered as it is in itself and apart from God. But
that is Nagarjuna's world, the Buddhist's Empty sublime! Aquinas
argues, as one would expect, that the empty world is somehow
impossible. It cannot be. So he introduces the omnipotent Will of
God to support it, structure it, colour it up and give it the objective
reality that he thinks we just know it has. And that is his proof of
God.

I am suggesting that the great difference between Eastern and
Western thought is that – in the past at least – the West commonly
had a strong doctrine of creation, and therefore a vividly 'realistic'
picture of the objectivity of the world, which rested above all upon
the Western sense of the infinite, omnipotent creative Will of God.
(Note that I am here including Islam in 'the West', as one should.)

Historically, human beings had to evolve their own consciousness and their own world picture solely out of themselves, on the
basis of their own sense-experience, their own continual linguistic
exchange, and their own trial-and-error striving and searching. They
had to evolve everything from within and amongst themselves. They
were always, and we too are always, inside our own faculties and our
own point of view. We never get any fully independent, authoritative
confirmation of our interpretation of the world. We see only *our*
world. With the help of historical and cross-cultural research we can
enter imaginatively into other human beings' world pictures and
learn from them, but we cannot jump clear of all human interpretation of the world in order directly to compare our interpretation of
the world with the way the world is in itself. Therefore the only world
we'll ever know is always already a contingent human interpretation.

These considerations suggest that one of the main functions of gods and spirits, and indeed of the whole idea of a supernatural order, has been to guarantee realism. God and his revelation of truth to us provided – or, rather, *seemed* to provide – the independent guarantees of objective reality that we in the West so much wanted. There is confirmation of this in the fact that in the major Early Modern philosophers who followed Descartes (and who included the British empiricist John Locke) God was still being invoked to guarantee the objectivity of our knowledge. The greatness of Hume and Kant lies in the fact that they first tried to construct a theory of human empirical knowledge *without* invoking the ancient Guarantor. They tried to stick to the principle that we humans really are on our own and have only our own point of view. Nobody but us uses human language; nobody else talks to us and tells us how the world is absolutely. Therefore the only world we can know is the world we make – *our* world.

The changeover from the old God-endorsed, God-backed programmes of knowledge, ethics, and religion to the newer exclusively human knowledge, ethics, and religion is enormous. It involves the death of God; it involves the end of *the Cosmos*, that is, the end of a divinely-established and guaranteed objective reality of things; and it involves our learning the truth of universal contingency in a new way that cuts very deep. When a theist such as Thomas Aquinas teaches universal contingency he means that all created things rest upon the Will of God. They are what they are because Omnipotent Will freely chooses and ordains that they be just so. Their reality is underpinned by God's power and God's constancy. But when a non-theist such as Nagarjuna teaches universal contingency, he means something very much more drastic. Everything is without 'essence' or a determinate nature of its own, everything is Empty of 'own-being', Empty of objective reality. Everything is utterly contingent and transient, including you and me and including also these words – that is, this present statement of the doctrine of Emptiness. Everything is Empty, and this sentence is Empty too.[1]

So there is an enormous gap between Aquinas's sense of everything's contingency and Nagarjuna's. It is like the gap between the lush, solid landscapes of Western art, and the evanescent lightness of Eastern landscape. Yet, curiously, there are things to say that narrow the gap considerably. The West was always aware of the possibility of atheism – that is, the possibility of a godless vision of the world. And when a Western philosopher constructed an argument from the world to God, an argument *e contingentia mundi* (from the contingency of the world) that needed to be not merely analytic but constructive, he was obliged to start from something like Nagarjuna's vision and therefore to admit (by implication) its intelligibility and its possibility.

How could this be so? The answer is that the old Western vision was always somewhat ambivalent about the reality of finite being. Since Plato real Being, like real Truth, had been thought of as timeless. There was a chasm between God's Eternal Being and the mere temporal 'becoming' of creatures. God was absolute Being, Being itself, self-subsistent Being. All reality was concentrated in God, who lent to the creature an appropriate degree of participation in his own divine Reality. Thus it was acknowledged that there is indeed contingent being, but creatures have their being not in their own right but only in their utter dependence upon the Will of God. In themselves, creatures are Empty – or, as Western writers say, they are 'nothing'. Everything is contingent. But if everything severally were contingent, nothing would exist at all, for nothing would have any being of its own. Therefore there must be some great non-contingent Being behind the scenes that is using its own infinite Reality to sustain everything else – and *that* is what is meant by God.

Thus Aquinas introduces the rather quaint conflict amongst the premises that characterises his Five Ways. They say *both* that everything is contingent *and* that not everything can be contingent, unless there is some great non-contingent Reality that undergirds everything. They say *both* that everything is moved, *and* that nothing can be moved unless there is some great unpushed Shover behind the scenes that first sets things moving. They say *both* that everything is caused, *and* that therefore there must also be an Uncaused First Cause, and so on. The curiously awkward conflict amongst the premisses of each Way is very noticeable; but still more interesting is the fact that perennially the Western vision of the world can't seem to get itself stated without having first invoked the alternative nihilist vision of what the world would be like *without* God. To this very day the conservative Western theist, whether a Muslim or a Protestant Christian, still customarily explains and defends his position by saying that without God as its creator, sustainer, and providential governor, the world can be regarded only as the product of 'blind chance' and therefore as being quite 'meaningless'.

Thus the modern apologist for theism still conjures up the alternative vision of the world that he is trying so hard to exclude. Without the creative Will of God to give everything reality and purposiveness, the world and everything in it are nothing but meaningless products of blind chance. Nagarjuna says that his vision of the world as Empty is bliss; but the Westerner portrays the same state of affairs as a nightmare. Why, you may ask, is the apologist so keen to frighten us? Why is he so haunted by the vision of an Empty meaninglessness? Leszek Kolakowski hints at the reason.[2] The Western thinker thirsts after a transcendent One, the Absolute. But the Absolute is beyond all the categories of our thinking: it is infinite and incomprehensible. As the mystic at prayer discovers, there is no *humanly detectable* difference between God and Nothingness. And that is why the Western thinker is so troubled. He's frightened by the thought of a world without God, but he's even more deeply frightened and troubled by the thought that his idea of *God* may be Empty and godless, too. Universal Emptiness terrifies him, and he is willing to go to any lengths to keep it away.

However, all this is water under the bridge by now. After the death of God there was bound to be a period of pessimism and a fundamentalist reaction in the West. But in time, as we have begun to understand Buddhism better, we begin to see the religious value of, and even to love, the very vision of the world that so terrifies the fundamentalist.

How this happened is as well seen in the history of nineteenth-century painting as anywhere else. In Rubens, or in John Constable, Western landscape painting is vividly solid and dense. But it got all its reality from the theology with which it was imbued: landscape spoke to us of Eden and the loss of Eden, of corruption and of our mortality. Take all the theology away, and the world loses all that solid reality and becomes misty and evanescent, like the Buddhist landscape of China and Japan. As God dies, the painter begins to paint not solid objects but only the play of natural forces and effects of light (Turner, Impressionism). Late in the century it becomes clear that the painter now depicts not the structure of the world but the structure of human perception (Cezanne, Cubism). Eventually, the painter depicts just colour, just light, just form, just painting itself –

as, analogously, philosophy turns to study just language. We are now happy simply to attend to the raw materials and the toolkit that we use in *our own* world-building.

So the disappearance of objective reality happened in art a century or more before we began to understand and to accept all its implications.

Empty radical humanism

The first industrial revolution helped to bring about a marked shift towards humanism in Western thought. It is typified by the work of Ludwig Feuerbach and Karl Marx in the 1840s and is well summed up in Marx's slogans: 'Man is the highest being for man', together with 'Man is no abstract being, squatting outside the world. Man is the human world, the state, society'.

Today the second industrial revolution, brought about especially by huge advances in communication and in information processing, is associated with a further shift towards what we have already called Empty radical humanism. It is a more radical humanism, in that the world is now fully appropriated to human beings. World building is indeed our characteristic activity. No other beings feel the need to build a whole world around themselves, and no other beings have language, the chief tool of our world building. A world cannot *be* a world without someone or some group whose world it is, and we see now that what we used to think of as *the* world is in fact just *our* world: we know of no other. There's only our world. Only through *us* does the world become world, because only by and in *us* does the world become described, theorized, known, and bright in consciousness. Such is the world you see and love so much, for the world is seen and known *as* world only in the brightness of our apprehension of it.

This observation prompts me to point out another reason why people have believed in gods. For several millennia it has been occurring to human beings that perhaps the world is older than we are. It is certainly older than each human being, for each of us finds herself born into a world that already exists, so that perhaps it is older than all human beings. But if that is so, then how could it have existed as a world before there was anyone whose world it was? The answer suggested itself that before the world became our world, it was created by and belonged to God, who then created us and handed it over to us, so that it could become our world. We see the handover taking place in the *Genesis* creation myth, and it is not cancelled by the sin of Adam. The effect of the Fall is to cause a delay: the full appropriation of the world to man can now be resumed only after a hard struggle. The completion of the long appropriation process is subsequently anticipated and symbolized by the standard early Christian image of Christ enthroned in Majesty, seated upon the firmament. Thus — as so often — we see that mythical thinking can be philosophically quite subtle and that Judeo-Christianity was religion that was always in process of turning itself into the radical humanism that is its goal.

To resume the main argument, the radical humanism that I am describing is a post-metaphysical, Empty humanism — 'Empty' in the Buddhist sense. The world belongs to us, it is our world, for it is only by being described and theorized by us that it becomes finished and bright — our milieu, the theatre in which we live and act. It is also worth remarking here that in contemporary theory of vision the very complex goings-on in the visual cortex involve regular consultations with the language producing area of the brain. In order to see, I have to be able to *tell* what I'm looking at: that is, I have to be able to put it into words. Just check now, and you will find that your whole visual field is 'bright' — i.e., consciously perceived, formed, and intelligible — because it has so much language woven into it. It almost *puts itself* into words. There are no spatial or linguistic gaps in the visual field. You can describe everything within your field of view promptly and in detail. And this happens because of the way the bit of your brain that constructs the visual field has taken such care to act in close consultation with the bit of your brain that generates language. So the world of experience is our own linguistic construct: our words build it and project it out around us.

But we are also parts of our own world. We don't peek into the world from some Archimedean point outside it. We are accident-prone physical objects within the world; we are agents and we are also patients. The same ceaseless motion of language that describes, theorizes, forms, and makes bright the world *also* describes, theorizes, forms, and makes conscious ourselves. Much more than we care to acknowledge, we are our own linguistic constructs. Talking about a novelist like Evelyn Waugh, who takes great care over the production and presentation of his image to the world, we are apt to say that he was his own greatest literary creation – but we fail to remark that the same is true of all of us. We are, we live, we represent ourselves to ourselves and to the world in our language – that is, in the flow of language through us. That's why I am talking about *Empty* radical humanism. I am proposing a theatrical view of the self: a person is not a substance but a role, a *dramatis persona*. We live and perform only in the show we are putting on: and when the show is over, so are we.

Not only the world, but we also – our lives, our thoughts, our faith and our values – are held within and formed by the ceaseless dance to and fro of language. It enfolds everything – including us. That is why humanism (the world fully becomes itself, formed, theorized, and 'bright', only in *us* and in our description of it, so that we are the only world makers, and our philosophy is rightly anthropocentric), this radical humanism of ours turns Empty. For we find that we must take a thoroughly naturalistic and post-metaphysical view of the self, as of the world. The consolation, as we will see, is that Emptiness is bliss. The more I understand that I am but part of the universal flux of everything, the more I am united with it. I begin to see the possibility of solar ethics and of a new kind of eternal happiness as I burn, burn out and pass away in union with everything else. To the 'Western' religious conservative, Evangelical or Muslim, the vision of the world and the self as Empty is nightmarish and meaningless. It terrifies him. But the more we learn it, the more we find it blissful. Call it energetic Spinozism, call it Empty radical humanism, it is very close to the strand in Western mysticism that loved to burn and said 'Our God is a consuming fire'.

The considerations that we have been bringing forward help to explain one of Nietzsche's most original sayings: 'The world is a work of art that continually gives birth to itself'. This is the doctrine of radical aestheticism: everything is an art product. The dance of language over the world, and through us, continually forms everything and makes it bright and beautiful. The Greeks were roughly right about form: the unformed is dark and chaotic, and the formed is 'bright' – i.e., consciously perceived and beautiful. And a corollary of this is that the age of the creative genius, the great individual human being who masters all reality in thought and remakes it, is over. The genius, and especially the genius in philosophy, religion or art, is a typically First Axial Age figure. In the Second Axial period we are more likely to put the motion of language, the dance of signs, first and to see it as creating us and all things rather than putting the individual genius first and seeing him or her as the master of language who imaginatively reinvents the world. Nietzsche, though himself one of the West's very last major geniuses, was entirely ready to accept this demotion, as one should be. The Buddhist tradition has on the whole done very well without autobiography, without the cult of personality, and without the hero worship of the genius in the Western manner.

Our humanism, therefore, is not Greek and heroic, but Christian, domestic and humanitarian. Remember that in Greek thought the Universal, the Form, was not just an average specimen but a perfect specimen of the type, We *still* tend to think that only a perfect specimen can adequately represent the type: thus in your bird book each species is represented by a perfect adult male in full breeding plumage, who looks very alert and bright-eyed. So for Greek humanism the representative human being is a nobleman, a hero, a warrior at his peak, a doer of great deeds. Greek humanism is close to hero worship, and knows nothing of love and compassion for the weak and afflicted.

Our humanism is unlike Nietzschean and Greek humanism. It is not driven by admiration for noble qualities but by human fellow feeling, sympathy, compassion. We are Empty, and individual human 'virtue' in the strong Greek sense is something too fragile and ambivalent to be believed in any more. In fact Empty humanism, which is modern humanitarianism, is strongly *anti*-discrimination. Our first concern is not to classify and rank people according to whether they are noble or base, male or female, old or young, black or white, healthy or handicapped, liberal or conservative, believers or unbelievers. Our political correctness quite rightly leads us to reject all these discriminations and instead focus all the moral attention upon our barest Empty co-humanity as the proper basis for ethics, for community, and for communication.

Attention to Be-ing

What is happening to the religious object? Does there need to be a religious object *at all*, any longer? Notoriously, postmodern societies are highly pluralistic. Life and the language are no longer dominated by a single religious system in the old way. Instead, we have some knowledge of half a dozen different religions that are all now settled amongst us, and there is also a pervasive secular climate of opinion that has become indifferent to religion. It is not surprising that the sacred has become scattered, so that many people find themselves feeling religious about personal relationships, about morality, about love and babies, about Nature, about art, and about life. When religious feeling has become so widely dispersed across the whole field of culture, we should surely consider giving up the idea that before all else it needs to be focussed around the worship of one supreme religious Object. If so, we may come to think of 'being religious' as an autonomous trait. Talk about believing in God and about 'the nature of God' could be entirely replaced by talk about a religious response to life and about what sorts of things turn it on.

In a post-metaphysical age no realistic account of the religious object can be made plausible, and none will be offered here. But there does remain a case for speaking of a religious object which is understood in a non-realistic way. For clearly we live in times when the old religious practices of worship, prayer, meditation and contemplation are in danger of vanishing altogether. Already they play almost no part at all in most people's lives, yet without them we are surely impoverished. How can something of the old practice of devoting religious attention to the religious object survive? In order to explain and justify religious practices, I will need to argue at least that religious attention should be turned this way rather than that, and that some practices rather than others are appropriate. So I will need some minimal account of a religious object. It will not be a distinct entity, and it will not belong to any transcendent order. It will be understood non-realistically. But it will direct our attention one way rather than another and so give focus to the religious life.

Three candidates are in the running. The first is God, understood in Kant's non-realistic way as a guiding spiritual ideal and perhaps as a straightforward personification of Love. The second is

Be-ing, understood in a Heideggerian way as a portmanteau word that fuses together and declines to distinguish between God's eternal Being and the finite, temporal Becoming of creatures. Heidegger held that the 'platonic' attempt to master Being in thought by making a clear distinction between two different levels or orders of being, one eternal and the other temporal, had been a mistake. We need to undo that distinction and wait for a fresh revelation of primal, self-giving, temporal Be-ing, mysterious, prior to language and unmasterable by thought. Be-ing is thus not a thing, but talk of it may indicate a way of making oneself receptive again, not to anything theoretically thinkable, but simply to the marvellous gratuitousness/graciousness of all existence. Finally, the third possible non-realist religious object is 'life', as that word has now come to be used in ordinary language. 'Life' is the ongoing process of the human world, the world of human symbolic exchange, the ceaseless drama – or soap opera – of human existence. It is our home and the milieu in which we live, in a dual sense: first, we are always inside the fact that we are biological beings. We see the world, or we construct our world, as animals with an interest in life. And second, we are always inside the continuously shifting world of human exchange which gives us language and shapes our thinking. The process of exchange continually produces and maintains the whole developing cultural consensus about meaning, about truth, about reality, about values, and so forth, on the basis of which we live. In this way life, like God in the old saying, is that in which we live and move and have our being, physically, socially, and spiritually. And the way people now talk about life suggests that it is becoming the acknowledged religious object. It is the first layer of the non-self: it envelops us, claims our allegiance, carries us along, guides and teaches us, and gives us our fate.

Thus there are three possible religious objects. *God*, understood to be simply Love personified, is already familiar from Christian literature and hymnody. Since most believers are not articulate metaphysical theists, and since they evidently no longer seriously expect God to intervene in the course of events on their behalf, it is arguable that the God of modern Christianity has already become an ideal god of this type – a personification of our highest values who is worshipped as such.

More important in the long run is the question of whether New Axial religion will attend chiefly to Be-ing or to Life.

It may seem that there is little difference here: for if we attend to *Be-ing* we are attending to the outpouring and the process of all finite existence (in which we all of us have our part), and if we attend to Life we are attending to the humming, ceaseless to-and-fro of human exchange in the social world (in which we all of us have our part). What is the difference? It is that for those who attend to Be-ing, the premier literary form is that of philosophy; whereas those who love Life see it best reflected in imaginative literature: poetry, the novel, and drama. That makes the difference look a good deal bigger and suggests to me that our Empty radical humanism is asking for a religion of Life.

This suggests that an old difference will return in a new form. The religion of Be-ing will be philosophical, reflective, and meditative. It will involve what I have elsewhere called 'moving-edge meditation', where we use animals or plants or gentle natural motions to help ourselves to attend to the passing of time in as narrow a specious present as we can manage. We try to listen to Be-ing and to recover the archaic wonder at its gratuitousness or graciousness. I need another portmanteau-word here that will capture that very strange thing, the blessedness of chance, the happiness of hap, the graciousness of the purely gratuitous. Happortuity, perhaps? We need a new word here, because we live in a time when so many people are oppressed by a sense of 'meaninglessness' and seem to be asking for a world that is thoroughly planned and meant. They are wrong: hap really can be very happy. Heidegger thought that the new revelation of Be-ing would be terrifying, but I find it easy, sweet, and female. It is symbolized by the Ingres painting of a standing nude woman who carries an amphora on her shoulder, from which a stream of water falls.[3] So, to think of Be-ing as our M/Other, think of a *chora* or womb from which pours a constant stream of pure contingency, perhaps like a waterfall. Our language meets it, is filled by it, forms it, fashions our world out of it. Being comes forward like a matrix (matter, mater): words fall and inseminate it.

By contrast, those who most love *Life* are young, active, and noisy. Their churches are city centres, tourist destinations, places of resort, and parades, where they congregate, meeting together for the purpose of meeting together (as an old joke has it). 'Crowd effervescence' is the Spirit they seek, the exhilaration of company.

Solar living

We are more long-lived and prosperous than human beings have ever been. Efficient economic management and social administration, together with modern medicine, have done much to reduce the uncertainty of life. But acute unhappiness is widespread amongst people of all ages to a degree that has been recognized only within the last two decades or so. Our politics is so much about efficient management and 'growth' that it cannot easily understand, much less propose any remedy for, the unhappiness of the very young and the very old. Our medicine does not do much better; for when personal distress is medicalized and treated as a pathological condition, it is usually not listened to and understood. Of psychotherapies, only 'cognitive therapy' recognizes that the patient has an *intellectual* problem. Of our religions, only Buddhism offers a serious and disinterested attempt to understand human unhappiness, diagnose its causes, and propose a therapy that, if persevered in for long enough, actually has some chance of working.

What is wrong with us? In Western language, we are much more troubled by metaphysical evil – that is, finitude – than by moral evil, or sin (a word we no longer need). Because we are finite beings, we do not and cannot experience or possess anything all at once. For us, everything has to be spread out and then taken in over a period of time. Thus our finitude commits us to transience; that is, everything comes to be and passes away, everything is already passing away by the time we have understood it: it all happens only once and everything comes to an end. It is transience that seems to prompt time dread: fear of contingency and mortality, fear of everything's passing away, fear of inexorable decline and dissolution, and fear of the loss of love, of rejection, isolation, and death. People fear what they call 'meaninglessness', which seems to imply lack of permanent religious weight, aimlessness, lack of remembrance, lack of recognition, and oblivion.

The hunger for public recognition is not new. In antiquity a man named Erostratus felt so oppressed by the sense of his own insignificance that on the birthday of Alexander the Great he burned down the Temple of Diana at Ephesus, one of the Seven Wonders of the World, in the hope of ensuring thereby that his name would live.

The Ephesians are said to have made the idiotic mistake of trying to frustrate his wish by forbidding mention of his name – an edict that was bound to be self-frustrating. And people like Erostratus are common amongst us. 'America', as it was envisaged by some of the early Protestant settlers, held out the hope of creating a society in which the common life of ordinary people would have such moral dignity that nobody would feel lacking in worth. Ordinariness would have an epic quality: that was the dream. Alas, what we see today is more often a frantic need for fame and 'respect', for any kind of escape from boredom and insignificance, and an absurdly trivial celebrity culture.

Why are people so dissatisfied with their own lives, and so hungry for 'meaning' – a very obscure use of the word: do they mean only that they want to feel that their lives matter; are they so hungry for meaning that they will go to any length and suffer any humiliation to gain their fifteen minutes of fame? The answer to the question has to do with the history of philosophy: for two millennia platonism devalued everything contingent, temporal, and mortal and taught us to seek 'solid joys and lasting pleasure' only in the eternal world after death. Then God died, the eternal world above vanished, and we were left with this life only. We found it severely devalued. What were we to do with it? From the late eighteenth century onwards we dreamt that it might be possible by political means to transform this world into a satisfactory replacement for the lost heavenly world, but those utopian political dreams have recently been disappointed in a final and fatal way by the death of communism, liberalism, and progress.

There is nothing for it. We should say plainly that what we most need is to learn to love life, just this life. We need to educate our senses and emotions, and we need to learn to understand our own bodies: most people are quite unaware of the extent to which a good visual education (for example) can be a source of great happiness throughout one's whole life. We need an immediate religion of transience – that is, a religion that does not look to the future but which verifiably delivers eternal happiness in the here and now. (By 'eternal' happiness I mean a happiness that we can turn to and rely upon however bad other things get to be. I personally associate this kind of happiness with sunlight.)

So we need an immediate religion of transience, of life and the passing moment: a religion that reliably delivers eternal happiness in the here and now. Furthermore, it has to be a religion that manifestly *works*: we have had more than enough of religious longtermism and postdated cheques. The religious life will not be a second, 'interior' life: it will be a specially intense and wholehearted way of committing oneself to and living out this life. There is no other.

The new religion I am talking about is of course 'solar ethics', which was introduced in chapter 6, above. In the period 1993–97 I also experimented with some other expressions such as 'glory', 'ecstatic immanence', and 'the mysticism of secondariness' to describe a way of living in which one is completely and unreservedly committed to the contingency and the transience of one's own life.

How does solar living solve the problem of death? In the old Christian platonic tradition people had a very defensive attitude toward life. One didn't commit oneself wholeheartedly to it; one tried to guard one's immortal soul from being contaminated by it. Life should be spent in preparing oneself for death: you purified your soul, you tried to keep it unspotted from the world, and you prayed for the Grace so to pass through things temporal that you finally did not lose the things eternal. Thus life was regarded as a difficult and dangerous test-track which you hoped to get round unscathed.

Solar living has the opposite view of the self and of life. There is no immortal soul and no heavenly world. We do not experience or pass through death: death is simply life's horizon. The self is a collection of biological impulses that seek as full and unified an expression as they can get. Culture provides roles we can play and approved forms of symbolic expression. So we live, and we obtain such life satisfaction as we can get by all the time pouring ourselves out into symbolic expression. We become relatively unified persons only *in passing*, and the self is like a role in a play: the character we impute to somebody is no more than our interpretation of her performance. As persons we have no being or life outside the show we are putting on, and when it ends so do we.

On this solar and theatrical view of the self, the best way to live is to live as fully as we can, and to put on as good a show as we can. Because the self becomes itself only in passing, it lives a dying life. It lives by dying all the time, so that the harder we live, the more death simply disappears as any kind of separate problem. Solar living is eternal life: it overcomes the traditional polarity of life and death.

The contrast between solarity and platonism is very marked. Platonism tends to be ascetical and celibate, whereas solarity is careless and spendthrift. Platonism always valued self-examination and inwardness or reflection, whereas solarity is extravertive and regards self-consciousness as a symptom of weakness and hesitancy. A good western Christian was supposed to spend much time worrying about the state of her soul, whereas a solar religious person just gives of himself all the time, and is very happy if he is able to say that he has no inner life at all.

How do we theorize this difference? Following Kierkegaard's interpretation of the Sermon on the Mount, I suggest that we should see solarity as 'immediacy regained after reflection'. The birds of the air live in *simple immediacy*. They have nothing to worry about: they are simply themselves and coincide exactly with their own lives. The heathen platonist lives in *reflection*: he has learnt to think and has thereby become a little detached from life. He considers other, absent possibilities; he hesitates, deliberates, and worries about the future. As ordinary language knows so well, there is an intimate relationship between thought and anxiety, mind and 'minding'. So the platonist lives an anxious life, suspended between two worlds, the world of sense and the world of thought objects. Platonism arose at a time when philosophy, and theory, and individual self-consciousness were just being invented. Plato's whole philosophy is something like an ideology of thought: it aims to show us what it is to become a reflective, thinking person and what great advantages one gains thereby. But eventually the time comes when we have sufficiently learnt that lesson and are ready to return into time, into history, and into our own biological life. Solarity is *immediacy regained after reflection*, and it ought to be able to take human beings to a higher level than they have reached so far.

Humanitarian social ethics

In the older Western tradition the term 'ethics' could be used to refer to a body of teaching about the good life and the way to blessedness. In effect, ethics covered much the same ground as what may nowadays be called 'spirituality'. So by 'solar ethics' I mean solar *per-*

sonal ethics, or 'spirituality'. With it I couple what I am calling 'humanitarian' social ethics.

By this I mean an approach to ethics typical of the past century or so. In the first place, it admits that morality can no longer be grounded in or appeal to anything 'objective' or extra-human. In the past morality was backed by the authority of tradition, or of God, or of a supposedly 'natural' moral law, or of a priori reason. Now we admit what is obvious, namely, that morality is human and is invented. Secondly, we differ from the utilitarian tradition in that we try to avoid appeal to anything psychological and/or culturally variable, such as, ideas of pleasure and displeasure, or of well-being and harm. Thirdly, we seek moral universality by sharply opposing any sort of moral discrimination between people on the basis of differences of race, religion, sex, age, rank, nationality, and so on. Our new humanitarian ethics is fiercely *anti*-discriminatory, and seeks to base moral action on nothing else but our co-humanity and the other's evident need.

By sharply repudiating all the discriminations out of which in the past people have constructed their world-views, their religions, and their ethnic identities, humanitarian ethics quite deliberately runs very close to nihilism. We cordially detest all the old absolutes and exclusive allegiances and notions of 'cleanness' and 'purity', and we reject the kind of fully developed religious and civil order in which people's 'identities' and their obligations, their beliefs, and their social roles – in a word, their social 'places' – are all prescribed in advance. To the contrary, we actively prefer and demand the wide-open, anti-discriminatory 'nihilist' type of society because it offers the maximal degree of spiritual freedom – which here means the freedom to posit one's own values, tell one's own story, and build one's own world.

In terms of the traditional Christian vocabulary, the distinction being made here is that between the Church and the Kingdom. Church Christianity, peaking in the late Middle Ages, aimed to provide a whole culture, a highly differentiated and ready-made religious order. Authority is in place already, truth and the moral law are published, rituals and social roles are all laid on. In short, everything is provided by Providence and backed by religious promises and threats. All you have to do is to fit in and play the part that is already scripted for you.

Kingdom religion, which historically was expected to arrive when the disciplinary 'Church' epoch came to an end, represents a thorough deconstruction of Church religion, with all the great distinctions and differences effaced, and the rules internalized or rescinded. Kingdom religion looks for a globalized and reconciled human world in which people are maximally communicative and transparent to each other, and in which everyone claims spiritual freedom for him- or herself and grants it to others. This is a nihilist world, because in it everything is wide open and nothing is predetermined. No doubt you will protest that some things – indeed, many things – must be received ready-made from previous generations, and that is indeed the case: but we refuse to follow tradition uncritically, and we insist that everything we receive must be treated as corrigible, negotiable, or reformable. In an anti-realist or nihilistic world everything is seen as a human construct, and everything is therefore open to being remade.

There will still be protests, because many people will say that a world in which everyone sees his or her life as a kind of art project, and is absorbed in developing it as such, could be a very selfish world. Not so: humanitarian ethics regards *any* fellow human's manifest need as giving rise to an urgent moral claim. Unlike the religious Right, it does not moralize or seek to limit other people's freedoms: but it tries hard to relieve the poverty, distress, or political oppression that presently limit other people's freedom to live well. Unlike so many other moralists, we see morality as being about freeing other people and not about attempting to control them. This is because in our view the happiest world is an open world and not a minutely-regulated world.

A corollary of our humanitarian social ethics is that we positively relish pluralism. We like the fact that the larger Western countries have recently become very multicultural and multifaith. We also like the new religious pluralism of those people who, following the examples of the Japanese and many West Africans, are personally multifaith. They don't see themselves as belonging to just one religion, and they do not agree with the loyalists: on the contrary, they freely admit to being like Wittgenstein, both Jewish and Catholic Christian, or like me, an Anglican who is partly Protestant, partly Jewish, and partly Buddhist. Why should we not regard the whole of humankind's religious heritage as our own and borrow from it as we please? There are no essences, and nothing is sacred: everything is human and as such is available to anyone. So again we must learn how to use the new Empty radical humanism as a spiritually liberating doctrine.

Chapter Eight

Emptiness

The Normalization of nihilism

Nietzsche strikes very theatrical poses when he is writing about nihilism:

> What I relate is the history of the next two centuries. I describe what is coming, what can no longer come differently: *the advent of nihilism* . . . For some time now, our whole European culture has been moving as towards a catastrophe . . . [1]

Looking back, over a century later, we wonder *why* he gets so excited about nihilism. He equates it with what I call the end of moral realism and the end of theological realism:

> Scepticism regarding morality is what is decisive. The end of the moral interpretation of the world, which no longer has any sanction after it has tried to escape into some beyond, leads to nihilism . . . 'Everything lacks meaning'. Buddhistic tendency, yearning for nothing . . . [2]

But why the excitement? 'The end of the moral interpretation of the world' was already implicit in the mechanistic natural philosophy of Galileo and Descartes. The sort of radical aestheticism that sees the natural world as in some sense produced by, and subsisting within, the imagination was already long-familiar to people of Nietzsche's own time. Even the dim English knew about it in Wordsworth. And again, the notion that our life is not objectively meaningful in some ready-made way, but that it is rather up to *us* to inject the purposiveness into our own lives, was not wholly novel even in Nietzsche's own day. Now, over a century later, most of Nietzsche's philosophy has become the people's common sense. His revolution is now their normality: they use phrases like 'live dangerously' and 'a free spirit' not as quotations from him but simply as stock sayings familiar to everyone. 'Buddhist nihilism' frightens nobody: everybody loves the Dalai Lama, and Buddhist meditation is widely practised. That one well-known Tibetan Buddhist figure recently wrote a dissertation on Nietzche in Cambridge indicates not only that the affinity between Nietzche and Nagarjuna can be recognized from both sides but also that both writers are now assimilated and canonical – part of our normality, even in Britain.

Against this background, it is now even possible to venture the view that nihilism is a friendly doctrine. Nihilism is (in the Buddhist sense) 'Empty' radical humanism; nihilism is pure religious freedom in a world in which nothing is 'absolute' and everything can be reimagined; nihilism is our own anti-discrimination; and finally, what Nietzsche calls the advent of nihilism is pretty much the same event that an earlier teacher described as the coming of the Kingdom of God. It calls upon us to live in radical freedom as if at the End of the World.

People like Dostoyevsky's Grand Inquisitor, who speak for some existing highly evolved religious system, always want there to be a fixed world order and a society in which there's a place for everyone and everyone knows his place. When such people are Christians, they are so orthodox that they dislike Jesus and hate religious freedom. It threatens their security. But today the condition of nihilism or pure religious freedom is getting to be everyone's normality, and we are beginning to like it very much.

Empty aestheticism

In what sense could a figure like Wordsworth think of the external world as somehow produced by and subsisting within the poet's imagination? I do not suggest that Wordsworth made any very close study of Kant and his German Idealist successors. Being English, Wordsworth was much more familiar with Locke and Hartley –, that is, with British Empiricism and the Associationist Psychology. And that was enough for his purposes.

For this tradition, all our knowledge of the external world begins with sense experience. The immediate objects of the senses are particular sense impressions. Sense impressions, however, are very fleeting and fast-changing. How do we make the move from them to our developed picture of an organised, independent world out there, with stable, persistent, physical objects, causal relations, the complex dramas of human lives and relationships, and other people's different viewpoints? How do we build all that, just out of the jumble of sense impressions? The mental faculty that does the image processing for us is traditionally called the imagination. It assembles impressions into objects, situates them in relation to each other, interconnects them, and so on. Because we all draw heavily upon our memories in order to interpret present experience, the imagination must be closely related to the memory.

The more we think about this, the more we see what a huge amount of work the imagination must be doing to build the world of everyday life for us and to keep us functioning more or less successfully within it. Returning to the young Wordsworth, who was both a visual person and a highly reflective one, we can easily see him contemplating the scenes of his early life and thinking *both* that the world he is looking at is obviously in some sense 'objective' and independent of his perception of it, and yet *also* that it is, and equally clearly, very largely a product of the poet's imagination:

> Oft in those moments such a holy calm
> Did overspread my soul, that I forgot
> That I had bodily eyes, and what I saw
> Appeared like something in myself, a dream,
> A prospect in my mind.
> — *Prelude* II, 367-371 (1805 text)[3]

In a note on the *Immortality Ode* that he dictated to Miss Fenwick in later life, Wordsworth recalls: 'I was often unable to think of external things as having external existence, and I communed with all that I saw as something not apart from, but inherent in, my own immaterial nature'.[4] From the more conservative standpoint of his later years, Wordsworth regards these thoughts as temptations, leading to an idealism that should be resisted. But he is wrong: it is quite rational to look wonderingly at the visual field and try to understand how it can be that what you see is *both* the product of a huge amount of processing and interpreting that is going on in the visual cortex at the back of your head *and* simply the external world. The modern psychology of visual perception still raises just the same puzzle, and just as acutely.

Aestheticism is the doctrine that compares the world with a work of art. The metaphor moves both ways: it is natural enough to speak of a major novel as an imaginary world created by the writer; and conversely, traditional myths may picture the Cosmos as a work of art created by the gods or God. And indeed in Western culture, just before the scientific revolution took off, it was common to speak of Nature as a Book written by God. Conversely, the poet's eye, making metaphorical and imaginative connections between widely separated areas of experience, may be seen as helping to finish the world by enriching and sharpening our perception of it.

So we may gradually give up the traditionalist idea that the Cosmos was created and completely finished all at once by God long ago and instead gradually come to think of our vision of the world as an imaginative product that we ourselves have collectively evolved over a very long period. Artists and scientists may be seen as playing leading parts in clarifying and enriching the way we all see things. They make new imaginative connections, and they introduce new vocabulary.

Since we have only our own eyes and our own point of view, we are always within our own point of view and have only *our world*. That is to say, our entire picture of the world has all along been developed only immanently and from within our own viewpoint. We can compare one human world view with another, but we can never jump out of our own heads in order to compare our world view with the way the world is absolutely. Realism is the doctrine that supposes such a comparison possible; but when we fully understand that the comparison is not possible and see that we can and do progressively develop and improve our world view from within and by debate amongst ourselves, then we may learn to stop worrying about realism. Things are what they are, and there is no need to worry about or even to think of the distinction between our world and the world or between truth that is invented and truth that is discovered. Thus 'radical humanism', which starts off by seeming an alarming and even paradoxical doctrine, may end up by being normality. We may even come to a point where there is no longer an unsettling and important difference between the traditionalist's belief that 'God made and finished the world long ago' and the late-Modern idea that 'We are continuously modifying and clarifying our account of the world'.

All that's happened is that we have made the change from a traditional-ist world view to the modern historical humanist world view and have amended our vocabulary accordingly. Notice here the interesting point that on *both* accounts we have a special relationship to the world, but that the terms of the special relationship have changed in the transition from the old world view to the new. On the old world view, God had set up a pre-established harmony between the human mind and the Cosmos: we were predesigned to fit into the world God had made for us and predesigned for our special destiny. On the new world view, we have in and through the motion of our language developed and projected out around ourselves a world in which we can live and flourish. As we steadily enrich and further elaborate our world, we appropriate it more fully to ourselves and get to feel more responsible for it.

Aestheticism, then, is a doctrine that sees artistic creativity as cen-tral to any adequate account of what culture is and how it works, of how we have built and how we change our world. The word 'poetry' comes from the Greek verb *poiein*, to make or create, and from the late eigh-teenth century onwards it came to be thought that poetry was close to myth and to music: it was the oldest form of language and the most powerful, with the greatest facility to express and shape feeling. 'To begin with one spoke only in poetry', says Rousseau.

The turn from traditional realism to language was already going on amongst the German Romantics in Wordsworth's time, but it did not touch him greatly. When it did fully come, the motion of language replaced Wordsworth's slightly old-fashioned faculty psychology. It is not the individual human imagination and memory but just *language* that forms our sense impressions, makes them intelligible, connects them together, and builds our world.

The difference between a human being and an animal is not that a human being comes with a lot of mental capacities that animals lack but that human beings have well developed languages which give them a world. An animal has only an environment of sensations, stimuli for at least some of which it has instinctive or learnt behavioural responses. A human being is different: a human being has raw sensations plus lan-guage that makes sense of them and builds them into a complete world. An animal may see a red movement; a human being sees *a bus*, stops it, and gets on it. An animal experiences a visual stimulus, but the human has through language the ability to apprehend the red movement *as 'a bus'* and so as part of a world.

Look at the visual field before you and see how everything in it is well formed, bright, and describable. You can tell – i.e., say – at once what everything is. Nothing is blurred or vague. Everything is bright and clear and properly woven together with no gaps. That's the action of language: it has already woven the sensory input into a continuous tapestry. While we were talking of Wordsworth and the poetic imagination, we noticed the close connection there must be between imagination and memory and felt inclined to wonder what, if anything, ensures that we all build very much the same world. But now we see that language has memory built into it and is of course common or public, so that people who belong to the same language-group inhabit a common world. Hence the very great extent to which the technical vocabulary of science, derived from Latin and Greek, is and has to be the same all around the world. That is why science is such a powerful globaliser: it builds one world for all nations. Hence again the possibility of forgetting the old worries about realism: the reassurance that the common language gives us a common world that can replace, and can cause us to forget, the old itch for objective truth. We can put the point this way: There is no difference that makes any difference between a public, common world and an objective world. The new private/public distinction can simply replace the old subjective/objective distinction.

Now you see why I am proposing the theme of *Empty* aestheticism. We have replaced the idea of the creative genius of the individual poet with the idea of the motion of the common language, which is much the same in Wordsworth, in one of his shepherds, and in all of us. If you have attempted creative 'thought' and have given it much effort, you may have discovered that the only way to do it is to relax and let language do the talking. Wordsworth's special gift was only that he was better than the rest of us at listening to the movement of language which went on in his head, much as it goes on in yours and in mine.

That is why I suggested earlier that the old notion of the creative genius is now somewhat out of date and why I am talking about *Empty* aestheticism. Are you shocked at losing the old idea of the creative genius? The consolation is that in place of it we get a very much more democratized notion of creativity. It is the common human conversation and the public currency of the language that is doing the world-building and is giving us our ideas. The creative individual is good at listening to what's going on and can make a little difference here and there, but the creative individual is not so much of a world leader as has sometimes been supposed. On the contrary, even an ordinary person can learn to listen to the running of the common language in her or his own head and therein has access to just the same sources of inspiration as those that the genius draws upon. You can do it, too!

By *Empty* aestheticism we mean that we are giving up the idea that everything needs to be traced back to the fiat of a sovereign creative Will, whether infinite or finite. Thus we would reject the currently popular notion that 'Shakespeare created the modern self'. No, not that. That sort of talk smacks of hero worship and does no serious explaining. It would be better to point to the cases of biological evolution and the origin of languages as examples of how – just out of the play of forces, just out of secondariness – astonishing innovations and very complex systems can develop purely 'naturally' and without there being any sovereign, substantial Self in charge. Empty aestheticism therefore notes that it is wrong to think of the world as barren, cold, and dead, for it seems that there is a spontaneous creativity working ubiquitously – in the gentle gale of Be-ing, in the play of forces, and in the continual production and modification of linguistic meaning. Anyone who tries to do creative work finds that her best ideas are gifts that come to her with no giver. And that is itself something that one can feel non-objectively religious about – that everything is contingent, gratuitous, gracious. For that, one may feel non-objectively grateful – though *not* grateful *to*.

Chapter Nine

Humans and Animals

From Descartes onwards, Western philosophers commonly found it necessary to include a chapter on the status of animals. Early Modern philosophy was much concerned to combat scepticism and provide intellectual backing for the new physics. A favourite manoeuvre was to make a sharp distinction between mind and matter, the aim being to show how the scientist was able to function as an ideal observer of the physical world-machine, working out its laws without getting himself personally too much caught up in the machine.

So far, so good. Mind-body dualism implied that, in thought at least, we could stand back from the mechanistic universe and represent its workings to ourselves. But then, what about the status of animals? Even before modern biology, human beings have always been aware of the very close bodily and behavioural resemblances between humans and animals, and even before Descartes philosophers like Montaigne were already asking themselves whether the dog that twitches and growls in its sleep before the fire can be dreaming. Do dogs dream as we do? Do they have subjective consciousness? Against this background the philosophy of Descartes seemed to present a dilemma: *either* we must say that an animal is just a body, a machine, *or* we must say that the dog has an immaterial thinking thing, a soul, inside its head just as we do.

Descartes himself decided that animals were just machines. It seemed to follow that animals have no feelings, and no rights; and that the very strong mutual sympathy that very often seems to link an animal with its human owner is an illusion, a weakness on our part. But by the nineteenth century people were becoming increasingly exercised about cruelty to animals, which was legally prohibited from the 1840s on. The notion that cruelty to an animal is wrong seems to imply that the animal has feelings, interests, and a point of view. It can suffer, and its suffering is a bad thing. Furthermore, during the nineteenth century people began more and more to see that we are not pure reasoners: all our subjective life rests upon the dynamics of the emotions, and emotional life is propositional – it can be read. (Hence today's new phrase: 'emotional intelligence'.) What is more, we read and interpret each other's feelings and desires very much as we read and interpret what our dogs are 'saying' to us. Not only do such considerations belie sharp mind-body dualism and the view that a dog is a mere machine and as such entirely different from a human being, they also show us beginning to move into a new world view which will simply not wish to distinguish between material and mental worlds in the former way. Instead we need to pursue the new questions about how we interpret or 'read' animal behaviour. To what extent do animals really *communicate* with each other? To what degree does a dog have a world and a world view? Just how complex are animal communication systems: does any of them amount to a language?

In earlier chapters I have been suggesting that an animal has only an environment of sensations but that human beings, and they alone, use language to *form* their sensations and weave them together so that they are apprehended as things in a world. Thus a human being has a world, which is the *theatre* in which she lives and expresses herself. So far, so Cartesian: I have said in effect that a human being has a world, whereas an animal is only an animate thing within a world. Not quite good enough, now. I am going to have to go a step or two further.

Animal expression and communication is certainly a good deal richer than anyone suspected in the past. For communication all that is needed is legible expression of propositional emotions, and to demonstrate legibility only appropriate behaviour in response is necessary. And all this is certainly *there* in the case of the more social mammals and birds. So there seems to be no doubt that we should now acknowledge that many vertebrate animals do generate and inhabit a rich *social* world. But their communication systems are not yet such as to enable them to go further and embed the social world in a larger, surrounding and richly theorized *physical* world. During the animal breeding cycle animals express themselves, and are distinguishable individuals to each other, in many and complex ways. Their social worlds may be very rich. But they do not seek to express themselves at *cosmic* level: they do not soliloquize, apostrophize, theorize, or pray. They do not express feelings in a cosmic and nonobjective way, by saying 'Damn it!' or 'Thank God!' They do not concern themselves about their animal condition in the way in which we worry about our *human* condition. An animal is not a puzzle to itself in the way we are, and the fact that we alone are such a puzzle to ourselves is an indication of our special status in the world.

To us, animals are innocents. They are like children who are still below the age of reason and are therefore unreflective. We like them because they are simplified versions of ourselves: relations with them are relatively easier to manage, and they can teach us things about ourselves. We treat them as if they were workers, servants, children, or companions, and we see their worlds as subworlds within our world.

Chapter Ten

Faith without Creed

The Joy of nihilism

The term 'nihilism' was introduced by Turgenev, in his novel *Fathers and Sons* (1861). It refers to the revolt against the outlook and values of their seniors by the younger generation in St. Petersburg at that time. Nihilism was thoroughgoing scepticism about existing institutions and especially about the received political and moral ideas and institutions. Nihilism was a call for a clean sweep and a fresh start.

In philosophy the term nihilism is mainly associated with Friedrich Nietzsche (1844–1900). He meant by it especially the doctrine that the world is non-moral. There is no 'providence', or 'natural moral law', or 'moral world order'. The cosmos was not made for us and does not give any endorsement to our moral, religious, or political ideas. It seems to follow that everything is permitted and everything is worthless: it makes no *cosmic* difference what we do. Nietzsche considered that it was this *moral* scepticism that mattered most. More generally, he was also a thoroughgoing perspectivist, who rejected the idea of absolute or objective knowledge. There is no Real World out there, whether of the kind believed in by Plato, or of any other kind. There is only the flux of Becoming.

Nietzsche distinguished his own 'active nihilism' – which says Yes to life and affirms the ability of strong-willed and creative people to create a new world, new myths, and new values – from the 'passive nihilism' of Buddhism, which teaches universal Emptiness – 'there are no substances, and nothing has any essence of its own: everything is contingent and relative'. As Nietzsche sees it, the

Buddhist is content to find peace in Emptiness, whereas he finds his own joy and consolation in being creative.

In the twentieth century nihilism often meant, after the two World Wars and after the collapse of communism, the doctrine that everything is discredited, that all the old ideas and good causes are bankrupt, and that our life is futile or 'meaningless'. After the First World War, artists who felt like this produced the movement called Dada. In the period immediately after the Second World War, Sartre and Beckett were associated with a similarly pessimistic outlook.

Finally, there is a sense referred to by Nietzsche and others in which all philosophers are apt to be perceived by ordinary people as nihilists 'who believe nothing and think that our life is but a dream'. This is not altogether surprising, for Descartes taught systematic doubt and questioning as the method of philosophy. It is the philosopher's job to question all the things that ordinary people take for granted. And in the last century or two this has often meant having doubts about God in particular. Anyone who has had a vivid and strong conviction of the objective reality of a loving personal God, and then loses it, finds himself or herself suddenly plunged into an equally vivid and strong conviction of being utterly alone in an infinite, cold, empty darkness. This is the Nihil, the Void, and if one is unprepared for it, it is like being damned or like being severely depressed. When in this state one cannot imagine ever being able to escape from it. But in time most people do escape and find they can congratulate themselves on having learnt a few useful lessons.

First, many or most of people's religious and moral tenets are comfort-beliefs, clung to as a defence against the Void. Such beliefs are defended fiercely: it is a sin even to question them. But any serious interrogation of one's own basic convictions risks discovering that some of them *are* just comfort-beliefs and must be got rid of. Perhaps this is particularly true of belief in God, which today has become so problematic. Serious religious thought today risks the Void all the time – so much so that in the end one is sure to be taught the great mystical and Buddhist lesson: *it is necessary to make a friend of the Void.*

This is how: if you have practised meditation or contemplative prayer a good deal, you will doubtless have learned that one method of thinking God, or just meditating, is by *un*thinking. One empties the mind. One thinks God by the indirect method of unthinking everything that is not God. One becomes stiller, quieter, emptier of sense and thought. Eventually one becomes emptied out, relaxed, and both alert and peaceful. God is an abyss, a shoreless sea, a desert. Because God is infinite, God presents no structure that the mind can grasp. God is a featureless Void – in short, *there is in the end no difference between theism and atheism*, and there is therefore no reason to fear the Void. It is peaceful as the blue sky.

As was noted earlier (p. 41 above), Leszek Kolakowski has written an essay about how the philosopher longs to find everything coming together in an ultimate metaphysical unity, *to hen*, the One, the Absolute. But as he comes to it he realizes that it is featureless and beyond thought, that it is unknowable – and it collapses. He is then plunged into what Kolakowski calls 'metaphysical horror', philosophy's version of the Void after the loss of God.

But I contend that in time we can learn to love the Void. We can learn to love the Empty, free-floating, foundationless, outsideless contingency of everything. We *must* learn this. Kierkegaard complains loudly about finding himself floating unsupported over thirty thousand fathoms of ocean, but once you have learned to float and are at ease in the water, there's no problem. The young Kierkegaard seems to be still a realist, who thinks that the only way to be cured of his fear of contingency's open sea is by a metaphysical guarantee that will anchor him firmly to the seabed. He wants to be saved by a Rock. But there is another way for Kierkegaard to solve his anxiety-problem: he must learn to stop clutching and let go. He must learn to love life and simply . . . float.

Two kinds of faith

Kierkegaard's complaint about finding himself floating unsupported on an ocean 30,000 fathoms deep neatly illustrates two very different accounts of what religious faith is. For the traditional realist – and the great majority of Christians and Muslims surely have been, and still are, realists – faith is the assurance of an unseen but objective metaphysical anchorage. For many people nowadays it is the feeling that there is *something* out there that gives our life the all-round Anchorage they seek; and this is accompanied by an intellectual life-history that amounts to a quest for objectivity.

For the modern non-realist, the special religious trick that is called 'faith' is the knack of letting go and surrendering control. Faith stops struggling and just floats on contingency. Faith, like zen, lets the arrow shoot itself. Faith lets be. Faith is often called 'feminine', as if it were like sexual submission and compliance; but that is a distinctly sexist way of making the point, because a man needs exactly the same giving up of anxiety and letting go in order to function sexually himself. So both men and women need to give up that little anxious knot of need to keep control and simply let be – which is another reason why we speak of 'Empty' radical humanism. Yes we are radical humanists, in the sense that we humans are the only speakers, and the only knowers, and the only fully conscious beings, and therefore in a certain sense everything happens in, through, and for us. Everything comes to a focus in us. To that extent radical anthropocentrism is unavoidable; but it is an Empty humanism, because we do *not* believe in the soul as a finite spiritual substance and a core self. Subjectively, the self appears only as a stage or an empty space across which language moves; and objectively, the self appears to others only as a *dramatis persona,* giving a one-off performance. That's all.

Briefly, then, realist faith is metaphysical. It is above all an intensely felt need and quest for an objective anchorage or foundation for our life. But in our post-metaphysical epoch realist faith is impossible and an out-of-date illusion. Non-realism is now our truth, and faith is a letting-be. It is the knack of floating freely and easily upon pure contingency. It is the knack of letting language run, signs dance, and the world flow forth. Faith is saying an easy Yes to life. Faith lets Be-ing be.

And I hope you now see something that I have myself suspected at times over the past decade but have never before been able to state clearly, which is that the system of thought that I have been developing piecemeal over the past so many years is only a rationalization. It is a religious philosophy that tries to elaborate, to explain, and to reproduce in the reader a cluster of ideas about religion and the religious vision in which I have at last found contentment.

In the past I have suspected and suggested that many or most of the great metaphysical systems – Spinoza's is an obvious example – are objects of the same kind: elaborations of the religious vision which the writer has found personally satisfying. Now I suspect that my own product has been something similar. It was presented in *Philosophy's Own Religion* as a systematic philosophy of religion and in *Reforming Christianity* as a proposal for religious reform. Here I have been presenting it as an induction course – as training in religious thinking. But however it is disguised and packaged, the basic message is the same: give up the quest for objectivity, give up the antediluvian idea that 'the truth is out there', and give up the desire for timelessness. Instead, say Yes to Be-ing, Yes to pure contingency, Yes to life, and Yes to the life-world as a self-producing, self-renewing work of art that forms in us and pours out of us.

Post-metaphysical philosophy, post-dogmatic religion

During the twentieth century Western philosophy gradually became fully post-metaphysical: that is, it gave up appealing for support to any other world beyond this world, and it gave up appealing to any point of view other than our human one. Gradually we became easy with purely immanent explanation and a more pragmatist account of our beliefs.

In the English-speaking world one of the last strongholds of platonism was the distinction between the *a priori* and the empirical – between the world of logic and pure mathematics and the world of fact. But when American philosophers such as Quine began to chip away at the distinction between the analytic and the empirical, they began to undermine that distinction. The last remnants of the platonic idea that beyond the world of sense there is a timeless world of pure thought began to fade away. By now we are pretty well accustomed to a completely immanent and 'outsideless' understanding of our selves, our language, and our world. I have described the new world picture under the headings of 'universal contingency' and 'Empty radical humanism', but contemporaries in analytical philosophy might well prefer to use phrases such as 'philosophical naturalism' or simply 'neo-pragmatism'.

Now how was religion to respond to this new situation? Historically we are used to setting religion in the context of a Two

Worlds cosmology. Religion is a matter of doing business with an invisible supernatural world. Unless we are outstandingly charismatic persons such as shamans or prophets, we do not have any direct access to the supernatural world, and must therefore rely upon various second-hand or indirect communications from it – prophetic oracles, inspired Scriptures, testimonies about miracles, traditional myths, rituals, beliefs, and so forth. Thus we have long seen religion in terms of a two worlds cosmology and a large apparatus of mediation that gives us a language in which we can do business with the unseen sacred or supernatural world. And you might therefore expect that when philosophy, and culture generally, become purely this-worldly, then religion too must either become immediate and purely this-worldly, because there is no longer any need for all that apparatus of mediation, or it must simply cease to exist.

What happened in fact has been something of a surprise. During the later nineteenth century, as rumours of the Death of God spread through the culture, religion began to take on new militant fundamentalist and neo-conservative forms. The novelty of this neo-conservative type of religion is shown by the novelty of the forces and ideas that it has reacted so sharply against: biblical criticism, darwinism, liberalism, secular humanism.

How could this happen? How was it that as the space within which traditional religion had operated began to disappear forever, a new and militant form of traditional religion was able to establish itself? According to the neo-conservatives themselves, the end of metaphysics has left a large vacant space, a god-shaped hole in our lives. This space urgently needs an occupant, because in a world of change and decay human beings desperately need something supremely real and objective to cling to and be guided by. So the neo-conservatives, whether they be Catholics, Muslims, or Evangelical Protestants, simply move into the vacant space, asserting confidently that now that metaphysics is dead there is no rival doctrine around with the intellectual strength to evict them. They have simply reoccupied an abandoned territory.

In explaining and defending their own claims, the fundamentalists and neo-conservatives must be careful. Their doctrine occupies the space of metaphysics but cannot itself be metaphysics; so they present it as a positivism of divine revelation and divine law. Their chief argument for it, if argument be needed at all, is simply humankind's great need for it and our own candid recognition, when we are presented with it, that it is indeed exactly what we need.

Now we begin to see why, as people in general have begun to understand that the Death of God and the end of metaphysics are upon us, the immediate religious reaction has been a strong reaffirmation of religious authority, religion as *law,* and the rise of militant fundamentalism. But the rhetoric of the neo-conservatives remains perplexing because, although they themselves claim to be post-metaphysical, they are so insistent upon the language of theological realism. They first accept, and profit by, the end of metaphysics, and then they introduce a strongly realistic form of theism which – in order to be intelligible – surely demands metaphysical argument to explain and defend it. What's happening here? The answer lies in their extreme revelational positivism: that is, they ground the objective reality of God in his own self-revelation to us. God himself has *declared* himself, and that is that. The objective reality of God, of divine truth and of divine law is all given to us within God's self-revelation in scripture. It is not to be theorized by philosophy but must be bowed to.

To this I reply that I for one still need philosophy to explain to me what is meant by such expressions as 'objective reality.' But, apart from that, authoritarian religion of the Barthian/ultramontane/conservative Islamic sort is, for me at least, not religion but politics. It is not about the liberation and the happiness of human beings but about the waywardness of human beings and their need for very strict social discipline. If I can tempt you to think that human beings can be made completely happy by a beliefless and purely immanent 'kingdom' religion of ethical commitment to life in the here and now, then there will be no need for the disciplinarian religion of the conservatives. It can be simply forgotten, because there will be no felt need for it.

So I insist that as philosophy and world view have become post-metaphysical, so religion must now become purely this-worldly and undogmatic. Perhaps the crucial point here is that, as we now see, purely immanent explanation is better. An external lawgiver is not needed. Even though the life-world is fleeting and contingent, complex ordered systems can evolve purely immanently and solely as the result of natural forces. Evolutionary biology gives beautiful examples, but the development of human cultural systems – and in particular, language – is an equally telling case. And when we have fully grasped the possibility and the intellectual superiority of immanent and 'bottom up' ways of understanding and explaining things, then the god-shaped gap is closed. There is happily no need to try to reinstate the religion of the past in a new and radically authoritarian form, because human beings are now ready to move on to a religion of pure expressive freedom – immediate, beliefless, and world-affirming.

Chapter Eleven

Against Religious Experience

By commending the regular practice of religious *thinking*, this book risks being thought to be in favour of religious *experience*. It is not – or, to be more exact, I am saying that it is essential to my position that we get clear about, and that we repudiate, a certain very common misinterpretation of religious experience.

What I am repudiating is the notion that 'the truth is out there': that there are special religious ways of getting hold of supernatural truths and of getting acquainted with supernatural entities. Just through our own subjectivity – so it is often claimed – we can have special access to objective religious Truth.

There are three classes of claim here. (1) The first is vividly evoked by the phrase 'a seeker after truth'. In troubled times when many people's religious views are in a state of flux it is common to encounter 'seekers' – people who are looking for the Answer: people who search for a truth that will resolve their doubts and give them peace of mind. These people seem to presume that the truth they seek can be discovered out there, and they make inquiries amongst various religions, other sects, helpful books, and persons with a reputation for wisdom or holiness. They may experiment with religious practices such as meditation or pilgrimage. Their behaviour and the language they use seems to be saying that what they are looking for must already exist and be waiting for them. All they need to do is to look in the right place for it. When they do at last find it, they expect to feel a little shock of recognition and satisfaction: '*This* is what I have been looking for all my life!'

This first group of *seekers after truth* are people who, as we see, have a very strongly objectivist or realist notion of truth and especially of religious truth. They see truth as something to be *found*, rather than *made* by us: something that we are entitled to expect to exist and to be, when we find it, exactly right for us.

(2) The second type of claim is that made by people who claim to have had some form of vision, or audition, or other direct encounter with a god, or a spirit, or a blessed saint. This experience, perhaps of Christ or of Mary, may have happened while the subject was in some special state of consciousness such as trance or while praying or meditating. It is usually emphasized that the experience came in some non-natural way: one heard a voice – but not in a way that could be tape-recorded; or one saw a vision or felt a warmth – but not in a way that could have been registered by a camera or a thermometer. Anomalous though it may be, the experience is utterly convincing, and it gives rise to a great feeling of certitude: the subject was able at once to *recognize* the one whom she saw. 'I *know*', she says flatly.

It is noticeable that what the person who has *a vision of the Blessed Virgin Mary* sees is recognizable because it conforms to the local iconography of Mary. People see the gods or saints that they already believe in, but nevertheless, they make strongly realistic claims. 'I saw Mary', they say, 'Mary herself'. In the cases of experiences of God it is harder to understand how the experient can tell for sure that his experience was an experience *of God*. But he *is* sure, and he couches his claim in strongly realistic language.

(3) The third type of claim is that made by the millions of people who say that they have encountered ghosts, monsters, evil spirits, flying saucers, aliens, or angels. The volume of testimony is huge, and the language used is once again strongly realistic. But the main consensus of society does not take claims of this kind seriously for two main reasons. The first is that scientists, along with the rest of us, have to develop rough criteria for deciding which hypotheses are worth spending time on. One cannot devote limited resources to a thorough investigation of every extraordinary claim, and there are many reasons for thinking that we need not spend time on the possibility that there are ghosts or flying saucers. The second reason for

not taking these claims seriously is that they are so very obviously influenced by culture and fashion. For example, flying saucer sightings (and even *photographs*!) are reported only from countries where people are buying cheap science-fiction magazines with pictures of flying saucers, looking just like *that*, on their covers.

We have described three sorts of claim to have had a special, paranormal, but *real* experience of a higher kind of truth, of a religious object, or of some paranormal entity. The claims have in common the fact that they are pressed upon us with great urgency and are described in vehemently realistic language; but the general consensus of humankind is that none of them is to be taken seriously. Religious *experience* as a way of knowing — as a way to truth — is a dead duck.

Why? Because *we* are the only users of language. Only *we* describe and theorize the world. *We* are the only producers of truth. The flying saucer, the Virgin Mary, the heavenly Voice don't come to us *from outside*: they are the projected conclusions of a largely or wholly unconscious process of religious thought that was going on inside *us*. They seem to be potent, relative to our lives, and to have an important message for us, simply because they are our own projected expressions. Thus when a Catholic girl sees the Virgin Mary, she sees an image of her own coming womanhood clothed in the local religious imagery; and when a somewhat paranoid small-town American sees a flying saucer, he sees evidence that we are all being watched all the time and that some great Event is coming which the government knows about but is concealing from us. And when some ordinary person finds the ultimate truth that she has sought all her life, she is relieved of her lifelong sense of being excluded from knowledge; because she never got the higher education she should have had when she was younger.

Thus religious experience, taken at face value and understood realistically, is invariably illusory. We are the only talkers: there is no ready-made Reality or Truth out there, and there are no non-human speakers out there. But if we turn the supposed 'experience' around and see it as autogenous and as a symptom, we can easily reinterpret it as the product of a process of unconscious religious thought and as saying something important and interesting about *the experient*.

These considerations should be enough to persuade us to forget 'religious experience', in the popular, uncritical and realistic sense of that phrase and instead turn our attention to the process of religious thinking. What is it? How does it work, and how does it benefit us?

In the examples just mentioned, the subject suffered from some strain and inner conflict. The process of religious thinking involved a search for a reconciling symbol. The thinking process was largely unconscious, but when the reconciling symbol was found it burst into consciousness as a 'given' religious experience. The subject felt relief and happiness. The adolescent Catholic girl who was worried about her own approaching womanhood found in the Virgin Mary an acceptable image of it. The somewhat paranoid countryman was encouraged by seeing a flying saucer to think that, in spite of what people say, his feeling of being watched all the time and his sense of some great impending Event was rational after all. The uneducated person who had a revelation of religious truth was comforted by the conviction that, so far as the greatest questions of all are concerned, everyone is equal and she is not hopelessly disadvantaged.

But all these cases were slightly pathological, so what is ordinary religious thinking? It is the simplest and most general kind of thinking that there is. It is indeed to meditate upon the reconciling symbols that religion offers us and through them to get ourselves together and feel happy. But more generally still, it is quiet and habitual attention to the gentle forthcoming of Be-ing, to the running of language, and to the dazzling brightness of the world. It is the most primal thinking and can be the source of the greatest happiness we can know.

Chapter Twelve

Just Thinking

hat is called thinking? is the title of a late work by Martin Heidegger, given as lectures at Freiburg in 1951/52, published by Max Niemeyer of Tübingen in 1954, and first translated into English by J. Glenn Gray (New York: Harper 1968). He also wrote several even later essays about thinking, such as *The End of Philosophy and the Task of Thinking* (1964). In this latter piece Heidegger is for once admirably succinct: 'Philosophy is metaphysics . . . Metaphysics is Platonism . . . With the reversal of metaphysics that was already accomplished (scil., before Nietzsche) by Karl Marx, the uttermost possibility of philosophy is attained . . . (Philosophy) has entered into its end.'[1] So, as everyone knows, Heidegger thought that Plato-based — or 'Academic' — Western culture was exhausted. We should seek renewal by returning into and rediscovering the primal kind of thinking of which we can learn something in the surviving scraps of the pre-Socratic philosophers.

What Heidegger is saying in these late essays makes a lot of sense. Our modern 'developed' countries exhibit an extreme differentiation of labour. Everyone becomes a specialist. Inevitably we have lost the archaic, holistic kind of thinking with which, long ago, human beings must have begun, and it may well be that we need to rediscover it — or something like it. For example, in science-based societies it is widely held that to get your account of anything right you must bracket off and disregard your own personal point of view and your own feelings. We have learnt to associate knowledge with dispassionateness, objectivity, and accurate representation. Result: too many scientifically trained people are mildly depressed, and too many people (especially males) tend to neglect themselves and have forgotten how to find the way to happiness. But archaic thinking takes its time, turns the object over, savours it, communes with it, is open to it, and is always concerned for the imagination and for happiness. Might it not be that Heidegger is right and that by rediscovering and cultivating a lost, archaic, and holistic kind of thinking we may be able to renew our religion and our culture?

The idea is worth pursuing – and I should say that what I am calling religious thinking is the same thing as what Heidegger calls just 'thinking'. But precisely because we have so badly neglected these matters for so long, it is very difficult now to speak and write about them accurately. Roughly, Heidegger says that Plato put us all on the wrong track by equating thinking with representing. One thought something by standing back a little from it and forming a *representation* of it in thought. From this act of self-detachment sprang every form of the split between the changing world of the senses and the emotions on the one hand and the timeless world of thought and knowledge on the other. Furthermore, it was this notion of thinking as the construction of an abstract diagram of the concrete world that in due course gave rise first to *science*, and then to the all-conquering *technology* of modern times, and the domination of modern life by incessant managerial demands for ever greater *efficiency*. Thus our history has been a process of gradually worsening alienation.

Religious thinking offers a remedy. It tries to rediscover and practise an archaic, holistic sort of thinking through which we can relearn the way to happiness. So far, so good. Now we need to go a little more slowly and try to work out what a primal, complete kind of thinking might be. Most people are not philosophers; how are we to interest them in just thinking? How can we explain what thinking is and why it is good for us? What is *pure* religious thinking, and exactly how can it make anyone happy?

Ordinary language makes a point for us here. Consider the jocular phrase about knowing someone 'in the biblical sense', a reference to *Genesis* 4:1 and other passages in the Authorized Version. This distinctive use of 'know' to mean 'have sexual intercourse with' was preserved in the Revised Version of 1885, and even in the Revised Standard Version of 1952 – no doubt because the translators could not find a better translation. Ordinary people like it very much, not just because of its mildly comical use of knowing as a euphemism for sex but also because of the more serious suggestion that knowledge was once something much more substantial than the mere skill with facts and theories that it is commonly taken to be today.

From this popular illustration we take the hint that the kind of new thinking we need is a thinking that *communes* with its object and not a thinking that *theorizes* its object (with a view, perhaps, to gaining some degree of *control* of the object). And, mindful of the fact that it takes two to tango, as the saying goes, we are talking about a kind of thinking that is not detached, but rather is *dialogical* or reciprocal: it involves the self in to-ing and fro-ing, giving and taking.

Very well: what then is the religious object? What is the simplest and most primitive term for the ambient otherness that bears us along and shapes us and with which we must come to terms? I answer simply *life*, using the word 'life' not in the biologist's sense but in the sense in which a novelist or a journalist would use it. *Zoe*, rather than just *Bios*. Life as the Empty, language-formed flux of things in the human world, within which we play out our individual roles. I am not returning to realism here. Life is not a substance or a thing; but then, nor are we. Life is an empty temporal flux of communication, a dance of signs. It is our milieu: we are produced within it, we join the dance, and we pour ourselves out into it again. In many ways, life is as God to us — which is why in our contemporary idioms we have come to speak of life very much as our ancestors used to speak of God.[2]

Now come some more difficult ideas. Religious thinking is archaic and holistic. Religious thinking seeks to avoid the customary distinctions between the self and the world, and between mind and body. For religious thinking the primary world is simply the world of life, the 'life world'. Our language builds only one world, so that our world, the life world, is in effect *the* world. At the very least, the life world is the only world that is on the syllabus for us. We have no knowledge of any other world and no reason to concern ourselves with any other world. I do not flatly deny the existence of any world but the world of ordinary life; but I do say that we have no access to any other world and no way of talking about any other world, so that we should simply dismiss the subject of possible other worlds, treat *our* world simply as *the* world — and leave it at that.

For religious thinking, the life world is the proximate religious object. It is not a substance, an independent thing distinct from us, for it is our life. It courses through us, claims us, demands our commitment, teaches us lessons, and is our fate. We should love it, trust it, and cast ourselves unreservedly into it. By that I mean that we should reject the old belief in an immortal soul destined to live in another world and should instead commit ourselves in an unconditional and religious kind of a way to this our only life.

Life is the temporal flux of things in the human world; life is a Beginningless, Endless, sempiternal process of symbolic exchange. Life is endlessly self-renewing motion. Life is like a soap opera, a baggy portmanteau in which the tragic and the comic, the infinitely serious and the utterly trivial are all jumbled up together. Since about the time of the French Revolution, ordinary life has been most people's main concern, as is shown by the dominance in our culture of the novel and other related forms – drama, opera, popular fiction, cinema, television, and so on. The consequence can now be stated in a short argument:

1. The life world is the only world, and it includes everything.
2. The novel and related forms are the media that most closely reflect and track what life is.
3. Therefore, 'the novel is our best totalizing medium', for it can accommodate everything.

The phrase quoted in the conclusion is from the late Iris Murdoch, who once suggested to me that I should try writing novels. I had to reply that I lacked the confidence or the talent, or both. Fortunately, plenty of other people have all the requisite abilities, and all the evidence is that – in the West, at least – most people's effective working religion is already the religion of life.

To take matters further, we now need a philosophical analysis of life. The best attempt made so far is Heidegger's incomplete work *Being and Time* (1927). For our present purposes, however, I believe that it is sufficient to distinguish three distinct aspects or modes of life. Each is ubiquitous. They are Be-ing, Language, and Brightness; or more fully, the forthcoming of Be-ing, the motion of language, and the brightness of everything in the life world. (Please remember in what follows that we need to avoid the traditional attempts to draw lines of distinction between the self and the world and between matter and mind. In using the word 'Be-ing' I am also avoiding the traditional platonic distinction between Eternal Being and the realm of finite, temporal becoming.)

By Be-ing I mean simply the continual, gentle coming forth of purely contingent and temporal existence. To explain this, we recall that in contemporary physics there is no absolute Void. Even in a vacuum at absolute zero, there are still quantum fluctuations, with particles popping into and out of existence – a neat example of the way the line between physics and philosophy has become blurred now, for in philosophy too there is now no Absolute Being and no Absolute Nothingness. Rather, in ontology we should think of a dance of possibility, a ubiquitous crackle of very faint white noise, waiting to be 'called into being', that is, to come out and be differentiated and formed by language. Be-ing is finite, temporal, flowing and gentle, language's M/Other. It is not real, it is not a thing, it is prior to language, it is what waits to fill out language and give it application.

By Language I mean the *motion* of language, language being a dance of signs and an *activity* of communication by which the world is continually formed, made bright, and kept in being. It takes a great deal of reflection to see how deeply our language interpenetrates, forms and makes intelligible, and so *appropriates* every bit of the world. Look at the visual field, and hear the language in terms of which you see everything. Look at yourself and your life in relation with other persons, and see how you and your relationships are *interpretations* produced within language.

Brightness is the most important and difficult idea, for it includes what is popularly thought of as 'mind' and 'consciousness'; but I have long taken an 'externalist' view of mind, seeing it not simply as our conscious awareness of the world but, even better, the world's own brightness and living beauty *for us*; so that for me brightness is public and objective. See it as *light*, both physical and intellectual at once. And divine, too. So the consciousness of our conscious experience of the world is not something subjective, an epiphenomenon of events in our brain cells, but something objective and public. Brightness is spread all over the world – the entire world – much as sunlight fills the visible world each day.

Brightness is the consciousness of conscious perception, seeing and being *aware* of one's seeing, and brightness is the beauty of the world, its fully determinate and shining character in our own consciousness of it. Brightness is the world's 'seenness out there', its objective intelligibility. One way to understand this is to think of the way language helps us to see with greater *clarity*: for example, when I know the names of all the trees, I see them much more clearly than I did before. They are more differentiated from each other. They stand out.

Am I clear yet about brightness? The Greeks were highly aware of the intense *shining* character of our sense-experience and to describe it used the word 'phenomenon', from *phainò*, 'shine'. A Press report recently described the case of a woman who luckily has had her sight restored after twenty years of blindness. She was amazed at the glory of the visual field, and cried out: 'My God!' If like me you were fortunate enough to have had a good early visual education, you will be similarly transported by the glory or brightness of things every day.

I have elsewhere suggested an analogy: as in Western Christian theology the Spirit proceeds from the Father through the Son, so brightness (or *Geist*) proceeds from Be-ing through language, which forms everything, makes everything determinate, intelligible, and *shining*.

We are talking about the task of relearning an archaic religious kind of thinking. Religious thinking is therapeutic. It is healing and reconciling. One finds oneself being included into a unifying vision of the unity of all things, so that one can say Amen, and be entirely happy.

The scheme I am proposing starts with life, which is the ongoing flow of things in the life world, which itself includes everything. We see life as a living unity of Be-ing, language, and brightness. Be-ing is non-language, a gentle outpouring of pure contingency, a whisper of white noise; language running everywhere forms of it a world of beings; and language's power to clarify (make *clarus*, clear) everything, and its reflexivity, somehow fills our whole world with brightness – and I, *even I*, cry out 'My God!', because I am awestruck at the dual lightness of everything. Everything, on this analysis, is light in the sense of being featherweight, non-ponderous, empty as a bubble, and also light in the sense of being clear, glowing, and radiant.

That is the new religious vision. Learn it. Cultivate it. To meditate on Be-ing, follow a new version of the traditional contemplative prayer by watching things pass. Attend to transience. To meditate upon language, do whatever will best help you to become more aware of language. Keep dictionaries on your desk and use them, do crosswords, write poetry, or simply listen to language by attending quietly to your own rambling thoughts. (I do three of those four). And to learn brightness, do everything you can to improve your visual and interpretative skills. Above all, look at the best painters — perhaps especially those of 1870–1914, Monet to Kandinsky.

Chapter Thirteen

Pure Religious Thinking

According to the myth of Babel, human beings were originally all of one people and spoke a single universal language; but their pride in their collective strength made God jealous, and he divided them into many peoples with many different languages.

The same belief in an original and founding unity and perfection also gave rise to the postulation of an original human innocence, rationality and virtue. The first human beings, it was supposed, must have been 'naturally' attuned to universal cosmic reason (the *Logos*) and to the natural moral law. By parallel reasoning, there must have been an original natural religion, traces of which may still underlie the various religions known to us today.

Until the late eighteenth century, the empirical evidence available to Western scholars seemed broadly to confirm this belief in an original natural religion. Its tenets were thought to include belief in a wise and good Creator; belief that the best way to honour and please him was by living a good life; and belief in the natural immortality of the human soul and a general moral reckoning at the end of time. By stretching the point just a little here and there this simple form of ethical monotheism could be portrayed as the original and universal natural religion of humanity, which still underlay what were then the three best-known living religions – the Jewish, the Christian, and the Muslim. Its rationality was confirmed by the fact that the major philosophies of classical antiquity, those of Plato, of Aristotle, and of the Stoics, had also taught it. It was known, of course, that polytheism had also prevailed in ancient times across much of the known world from Iceland to India, but one could well imagine that polytheistic religious systems had arisen by the corruption of an original monotheism.

Thus, until the eighteenth century or so, Biblical myth and secular knowledge seemed to tell much the same story about the religious history of humankind. There were a few dissenting philosophers such as Hobbes and Hume, but belief in what was called 'Primitive Monotheism' was so entrenched that it could still be defended by a serious scholar (W. Schmidt) as late as the 1920s.

Against this background, 'pure' or universal religious thinking was the sort of philosophical reasoning by which theologians sought to establish the major tenets of natural theology. It collapsed, mainly during the period 1760–1800, as a result of philosophical criticism of it by Hume and Kant; but then the nineteenth century brought a great increase in knowledge both of the great religions of Asia and of the religion of tribal societies; and in addition the triumph of darwinism ended the old habit of seeing history as a story of decline from an original state of perfection.

Today 'natural religion' and 'natural theology' are stone dead. Students of religion are agreed that all actual religion is 'positive' – that is, tied to a particular people, a particular language, a particular cultural tradition, and particular founding myths. It is a mistake to look for and expect to find cross-cultural and universal religious truths.

In that case, why am I talking about 'pure' – i.e., universal – religious thinking? Why am I trying to revive a thoroughly exploded idea?

The answer is of course that at the end of the First Axial Period modern technology is rapidly creating a single world culture and economic system. Airlines, banks, hospitals, and universities are already much the same everywhere, as are power stations, road transport and environmental debates. The extent to which there is already a single world culture is great enough to have consigned the older local cultural traditions to the tourist trade and the history books. The Second Axial Age must, inevitably, try to develop a new and *single* global moral and religious vocabulary.

In this matter we have already had considerable success on three fronts. Liberal democratic politics is either already established or urgently desired almost everywhere. The Universal Declaration of Human Rights (1948) has done much to establish the moral authority of the idea of individual rights, and the great international humanitarian charities have everywhere introduced the idea that our common humanity makes a moral claim that overrides the historic differences between individuals and between peoples.

We are already well on the way to creating a world moral vocabulary: what about the parallel task of creating the first truly universal *religious* vocabulary? Here the news is not so good. Despite the historical evidence of the extent to which in the past the major faiths have borrowed from each other, the faiths have tended to become exclusive, each asserting its own completeness and denying that it has anything to learn from the others. Sometimes it is alleged that all the faiths share an interest in affirming 'spiritual values' and in trying to resist the advance of something called 'materialism', but I do not need to repeat here my objections to the spirit/matter contrast. Others join the present Pope in seeing belief in God as the essence of religion and in therefore being willing to make friendly overtures to Islam, while detesting Buddhism. To this I reply that from the religious point of view Buddhism is the most intellectually formidable and challenging of the faiths and the one above all which we must reckon with.

So far we have made negligible progress in developing a world religious vocabulary. Why? Because we still think in the terms of the First Axial Period, and we still cling to the various local religious traditions that have come down to us from that epoch. In First Axial times human knowledge was very incomplete; indeed, by today's standards it was almost non-existent. The world was only very partially explored and hardly at all theorized. People knew little of the causes of things, instead supposing themselves surrounded by mysteries and non-human Powers. We simply had not as yet come anywhere near to appropriating the world fully to ourselves and making it *our* world. The most we could imagine was that *God* had appropriated the world to himself and so had made it *his* world – and we might imagine that perhaps one day God would delegate his lordship over the world to us.

Today the situation is entirely different. Anyone with a good historical eye and a scientific education now sees and inhabits a world entirely appropriated to human beings. Our language and our theory

have formed and brightened everything in sight. There are virtually
no mysteries left. We don't need to postulate any supernatural order
nor to develop a realist theology. We are ready for a new understanding of the human situation and a new *universal* religious outlook. I
am suggesting that the new religious consciousness will focus around
what I call Emptiness (everything is Empty; behind the flux there is
no metaphysical order that holds everything together) and Brightness
(the mind is made of language; language is spread over and interwoven with everything; and everything is therefore glowing and radiant in our consciousness of it). The religious outlook of the new
period will be what I call 'Empty radical humanism': not a humanism of pride and strength but a *religious* humanism of love and pity
for the human in its very transience and weakness. To think in these
terms is to engage in *pure* religious thinking and to be developing
what may gradually become the first fully global religious outlook.

Chapter Fourteen

Be-ing, Language, Brightness

Speaking religiously rather than philosophically, there are three great wonders – be-ing, language, and brightness.[1] Each is somehow irreducible. Each is so big that it's ubiquitous and so near that it's hard to get hold of. We have to go over them all afresh, in the hope of getting them right.

By be-ing I mean the forthcoming of everything. It is the way everything gently and uncomplicatedly comes to be in time, remains a while, and then passes away. Be-ing is always temporal and always contingent. It just *happens*, 'hap' being chance or contingency. Pure unformed Be-ing, prior to language, cannot be talked about and may (following Heidegger) be written as ~~Be-ing~~, 'under erasure'. I compare it with 'quantum fluctuations in the vacuum' in our contemporary physics: there is no absolute nothingness, for even in the void at absolute zero there is still a trembling of possibility, as particles pop into existence and out again. So Be-ing prior to language may be pictured mythologically as a shivering and a quivering that waits to be called out into determinate being by language. Be-ing is what mysteriously 'puts fire into the equations', says Hawking, but the metaphor that springs to my mind pictures words as like deflated balloons and Be-ing as a gentle gale, a squirt of helium from a gas tap that fills the words out, makes them solid and three-dimensional.

An older story divided all reality between two sorts of being. There was eternal, necessary Being, and there was also the whole created world of finite, temporal, and contingent beings, often called the word of 'becoming'. This world of created things was in itself unreal. It would vanish instantly if Eternal Being stopped willing it and upholding it. But the idea that Eternal Being gives rise to and upholds a complex changing temporal world, with finite beings all coming into being at different times, is incomprehensible to us. How can we think of something temporal as issuing from its Eternal Ground at one time rather than another? We can't: the whole business is unthinkable and/or indescribable.

The new picture of Be-ing as always contingent and temporal is very much simpler and clearer than the older picture and is associated with a major revaluation of everything. In the old picture the division between Eternal Being and mere temporal becoming was paralleled by a very important religious division of the human life world into the two realms of the sacred and the profane. Everything that had to do with our relationship with Eternal Being was put into the sacred sphere and fenced about. Everything else was outside the fence – i.e., the temple or 'fane' – and thus was 'profane' (or common, or secular). There was at least a tendency to attribute infinite intrinsic value to whatever was Sacred and almost no value at all to merely profane things. But at the Reformation the old Sacred/Profane frontier was considerably disturbed, as Luther and others strove to attribute positive religious value to secular life, secular roles, and secular callings. More recently, since the late nineteenth century the line between sacred and profane spheres has become almost completely erased, with the result that the sacred has become scattered across the whole life world. Religious feelings of love and awe may nowadays be prompted by very diverse events and experiences such as, for example, visiting Antarctica, seeing your own child being born, and watching insects.

So it has now come about that the emergence of the newer account of Be-ing has coincided with a revaluation of everything that is fleeting, finite and contingent, and a turn to *Life* as the new religious object (or 'non-objective object', because life is not a substance or thing separate or distinguishable from us). This new and intense love for the most ephemeral and transient things has a number of precedents in religious literature: one that I like to cite is a typical piece of his sudden eloquence in which Dogen (in thirteenth-century Japan) attributes Bodhi-mind to 'ocean-spray, bubbles and flames'.[2]

In talking about Be-ing, then, we are talking about the cultural revolution that is now enabling us to recognize, accept, and find pos-

itive religious value in the transience of everything, including ourselves and each of those we love.

By language I mean the dance of signs, the continuous process
of symbolic exchange between people, the humming communications network of which the human life world consists. I mean also to
invoke the vast strange and multi-dimensional world of linguistic
mean-ing — and I am hyphenating mean-ing, like be-ing, because
mean-ing is a process too. We need to make this point because for so
long European intellectuals studied only dead languages — Latin,
Greek, and Hebrew — and failed to grasp the way the transactions of
life are carried out and the life world is produced and formed by the
motion of living language.

My suggestion that the ambient life world in which we live, the
'physical' world, is produced all the time by the motion of language
may seem paradoxical. Let me spell it out a little. I'm saying that the
structures of the life world reflect the parts of speech. For example,
the space and time of the world of linguistic meaning logically pre-
cede and produce the Euclidean space and Newtonian time of everyday life. Consider for example how the whole structure of space and
time is already implicit in our use of the prepositions to conjure up
the three dimensions of space — from top to bottom, from front to
back, and from left to right — and the one dimension of time, before
and after, sooner and later. Kant described space and time as 'forms
of our outer intuition'; I'm saying that we think in language and that
our language imposes upon the world of experience certain conceptions of space and time, and so on. We see things in terms of nouns
and adjectives, verbs and adverbs, and so on. And I have argued elsewhere that it is just *because* we see things and build our world of experience in terms of language that a running commentary given by a
skilled, quick radio commentator conjures up such a vivid *picture* in
the 'minds' of his audience. (Incidentally, the example *also* shows
that members of the same language group all build the perceived
world of experience in much the same way and out of much the same
words.)

What is the raw material that language orders? It is what Kant
calls 'the manifold of intuition' — white noise, crackles and splutters
of sense-experience. More we can't say — in fact, we can't really say
even that much. It would be better to produce the text of a
Shakespeare play, and say: 'Look! There's nothing here but language

95

being batted back and forth. But all of human life is here. Read this, and it will conjure up a whole world for you.'

Once again I want to say that this doctrine is nowhere nearly as far-fetched and paradoxical as people's first reaction to it seems to imply. That the natural world is made by language and is full of signs is scriptural doctrine for Jews, Christians, and Muslims. In Renaissance thought at the time of the scientific revolution, it was common to see the physical world in terms of language and symbolic associations. Then in the early scientific doctrine of the Two Books it came to be said instead that the Book of Nature is written in the language of numbers; and indeed mathematics is itself a collection of specialized sub-languages. Physicists still see the physical world as a complex mathematical pattern into which somehow a mysterious non-mathematical 'spark' or 'fire' has been breathed and has actualized it all.

A last little argument: we have argued that all our ideas about space and time are produced by – are implicit in – the way we use language, and especially the prepositions and the tenses of verbs. This example explains what was meant when we earlier advocated a spirituality (i.e. a customary religious practice) of 'listening to language'. As they say, *It's all there!* The language running in your head already has all philosophy and all wisdom latent within it. The very *fons et origo* of all things is running like a leaky tap in your head all the time, and you have only to listen to it.

Be-ing is wonderful but very elusive. Language is wonderful by being so overwhelmingly rich, complex, creative, and close to us. But brightness is aesthesis itself, aesthetically so great that it is like the divine Glory, which was a light so dazzling that it blinded one and produced an effect of darkness. Brightness is so difficult that even the British Empiricist philosophers, who spent so much time thinking and writing about visual experience, somehow kept on missing it.

To begin with, I make three points:

1. In ordinary sense experience, I don't just see a green patch: I am *conscious* of the greenness I see.
2. Except in the case where I have a migraine, my sense experiences are not located in my brain, but are in various degrees referred outwards. Thus if I prick my finger, I feel the pain not in my brain, but in my finger; and if I hit a hockey ball, I feel the impact not just in my hands but out at the end of my

hockey stick. Similarly, I hear sounds at certain distances and in certain directions (the notable exception here being the case of a personal stereo, like a Walkman, the sound of which is heard in the space of one's skull).

3. I rarely experience isolated visual data. My visual experience is *always* (at least while my eyes are open) the conscious seeing of a complete world, with no gaps in it.

The basic conclusion to which these three observations point us is that our experience of things is not located in the brain but out in the place to which it is referred. When I see something, I don't see a picture of it in my skull: I see it out there, in the 'external' world.

Here we note that the manner and the extent to which we refer experiences outwards varies a good deal with different senses. I experience *tastes* in my mouth but am doubtful about referring tastes out to the classes of object that cause them. I experience *odours* in my nose, but when I sniff things I am a little bolder in referring the odour to the aromatic object. *Temperature* is rather unspecific, and most of the time we feel it bodily and attribute it to the environment generally: it's hot, it is a hot day, the weather is warm, it's hot in here. But I do refer *radiant* heat outwards, with confidence.

– And so on: now I can state a general theory that accounts for this odd collection of data. Human beings urgently need to build a world around themselves to inhabit and be guided by, and being highly social animals they urgently need to build a *common* world. The data of the senses are very obscure and miscellaneous indeed: how on earth were we to build a common world out of them? For practical reasons, hearing and language had to come first. Over the millennia we gradually experimented, discovered, and made an established custom of the best way selectively to refer outwards and to interpret our sense experiences, so as to assemble them into the most coherent picture of a common world that we could find. Our culture – that is, our common language – teaches each one of us how to select, interpret, project out, and assemble our sense experiences so as to construct our common world. Notice that every natural language is a complete language, because every human group has the same need to build a complete common world.

It has all been pragmatic, and it has all depended upon language. The upshot is the world we have, common, made by language, mind dependent, and above all *bright* in consciousness. To quote earlier slogans of my own, Your field of view is full of your consciousness; Your mind is out there, in front of your face; *All this*, before you, is what fills your thoughts.

In a way, our ancestors understood this point: it is suggested by the Aristotelian maxim *mens est quodammodo omnia*, the mind is in a manner all things. But it has all been made very much more vivid by the enormously enhanced differentiation, theorizing, and appropriation of the world since the rise of modern science. Now, the experienced world is to a previously unprecedented degree *ours only*. It has been made very highly determinate by having been described and theorized so minutely, and this makes it quite dazzlingly *bright* in our consciousness of it. Its glory astonishes me every day.

A further point now needs to be added. A theory of consciousness and of the world of experience close to mine has recently been published by Max Velmans in his *Understanding Consciousness*.[2] But Velmans is a realist. He says that the mind-dependent world of experience that we project out is 'a representation' of a real three-dimensional world, independent of mind that *also* exists out there and in the same place. But it is immediately obvious that we can know only the mind-dependent world out there that we build. We have no reason at all to postulate in addition a 'real' world beyond it, and no way at all of comparing our 'representation' with the alleged real world behind it. So the postulated real world is redundant and should be dropped. The result is my 'radical humanism', which is going to be Empty (for we ourselves are parts of the world we build!) but which is very bright, very bright indeed. And the core of the philosophical and religious position I am trying to describe is this intimate conjunction of utter Emptiness with the most dazzling Brightness.

A painter illustrates the point. He was one of the least self-concerned and self-revealing of artists, and he caught the brightness of our late modern experienced world perhaps better than anyone else before him had done. It was said of him that 'Monet is only an eye; but what an eye!'

To be happy about the Emptiness of the self and the brightness of the world of experience is a postmodern and partly secularized version of the theist's forgetting of the self in the vision of God's glory.

Chapter Fifteen

Emptiness, Brightness, Truth & Reality

Pragmatically (but no more than that), the apparent world, the world of everyday life that we have gradually learnt to build around ourselves, does work and to that extent has a degree of truth and reality. It is only an interpretation of selected bits of the complex crackle and splutter of sense experience, but for most of the time it works very well. We have no alternative to it, so that it is not surprising that most people, most of the time, take it all for granted. With it we can find our way around, satisfy our desires, accomplish our projects, and even manage − if we try hard enough − to rub along together contentedly. It all works just fine. True, the sharp eyed amongst us notice little anomalies and oddities in it here and there, but that is why we do science: we develop scientific theory in order to darn over the little holes and rifts in the life world.

Pragmatically (but no more than that), the world of scientific theory that we have gradually developed in order to rectify the various little faults and anomalies in the life world does work − and to that extent it too appears to have a certain degree of truth and reality. So successfully has it made our world picture more elaborate and consistent that it has already given us a range of very powerful technologies. And there will be much more to come.

However, both the everyday life world and the world of scientific theory are human constructs, made of language that forms and joins up selected bits of sense experience in order to create as consistent and manageable a common world picture as we can get. It all works well, and as I have been stressing it can often strike us as quite dazzlingly bright and beautiful: but it is only a world of phenomena (phenomena are shinings, showings-up, or appearances) that have been joined together by casting a net or veil of language over them. It is all beautiful, and it does work: that is why so many scientists make the entirely understandable mistake of being realists about their theories, by claiming objective or dogmatic truth for them. But neither the everyday life world nor the world of scientific theory has or can possibly have quite the old sort of dogmatic or metaphysical reality. *That* sort of reality used to come from the creative Will of God or from the metaphysical order and belonged – *nota bene* – to an age when there was no rapid change in theory, because human beings did not yet have any powerful research techniques. Today we live in the great age of man-made knowledge. We have highly effective research techniques, rapidly developing scientific theory, and rapid change in our world picture. The age of metaphysics, when knowledge and world picture were relatively very stable, is long past. Result: nothing is or can be quite as solidly and immoveably *real* as it formerly seemed to be.

Today, our scientific theory is a huge but wonderfully lightweight net that we have cast over the world of appearances (= showings-up, sense data). The combination of net and shining scraps produces a very large continuous and colourful arras or hanging tapestry – our work of art.

Now, how do we interpret the metaphor of a painted veil or an arras? To start with, keep saying to yourself: 'But there's nothing behind it'. When you have fully absorbed that, move on to a more exact statement of the position: 'It isn't the sort of thing that can have something "behind" it: it has no "behind". Being what it is, it is complete *as* it is'. Now spend enough time on that point to have absorbed it fully and then go on to the next and more advanced stage: 'The arras has no out-back, and for that matter has no in-front either. We don't observe it from some privileged vantage point outside and above it. It is the world of ordinary language and everyday life, a world that has no outside at all. You and I are *part* of the tapestry. We are woven into it, too. We can't be any more real than the rest of it is.'

Everything is on the painted veil, everything is made of empirical scraps joined together by a net of interpretations, and we *conjec-*

ture each other in such a way that I'm your interpretation of me and you're my interpretation of you. The human, too, has lost its former metaphysical weight and now shares in the relative lightness of everything. We, too, you and I, are caught up in the general Emptiness and brightness. What do we make of that?

Chapter Sixteen

Emptiness, Brightness & Humanity

Greatness and littleness

We have arrived at an odd paradox, a new and hyperbolical version of the old paradox of human greatness and littleness that was most famously described by Pascal and by Alexander Pope. In the new world picture we've been describing, the human being is more central, and more necessary in order to complete and crown the world, than ever before. It is only with us that language arrives and only with language that the world at last becomes fully described, theorized, determinate, finished, and beautiful. And there is more yet to be said, for language is highly reflexive, easily bent back upon itself, and marvellously good at talking about itself – which means that the reflexivity of language becomes the basis for our self-consciousness and our awareness of the world's dazzling brightness in our *conscious* awareness and knowledge of it.

This order of exposition makes clear why only two or three years ago I put 'Man' where I now put brightness, the word 'Man' signifying the human knowledge and consciousness in which alone the world finally becomes fully and beautifully its own finished self. Thus indeed we humans are collectively the world subject, in whose eyes the world fully and finally becomes itself as world and recognizes itself.

So much for the ratification of human greatness; but it is also a confirmation of human littleness, because the story of how human beings and their world have become completely appropriated to each other is of course *also* the story of how we have gradually been forced

103

to give up the old dream that a bit of us doesn't belong in this world and is destined to live eternally in a better world elsewhere. We now recognize that we are as transient and insubstantial as everything else – and must be content with that.

It was formerly claimed that God 'has put eternity into man's mind'. But we have retreated from that position in a series of stages. Once, it seemed that we must be *capax infiniti* (capable of the infinite), because we could live in intimate consciousness of and fellowship with the Infinite and Eternal God. More cautiously, it seemed that there must be something of eternity in us because we are capable of grasping the timeless *a priori* truths of logic and mathematics. Most recently still, it could seem that there is something of eternity in us because in our moral experience we find ourselves constrained by and aware of something that transcends time and remains itself unchanged. But step by step our growing historical awareness has forced us to recognize the deep implications of the fact that religious feeling, that logic and mathematics, and that moral experience – *all* of them are human, and all have human histories.

Slowly we have given up the last traces of belief in 'life after death' and have become ready to accept and affirm the obvious, which is that we are as ephemeral as everything else is. Collectively we matter a great deal, but individually we are simply transient and don't matter as much as we used to think we did.

Is this paradox of human greatness and littleness, the paradox of '*Empty* radical humanism', itself a matter of great religious concern? And if so, how do we resolve it? I answer, in general, that the knowledge of our mortality and universal transience adds a touch of Angostura bitters, a touch of anguish, to our lives; but on reflection the angostura is a tonic, an enhancer, and we wouldn't be without it. We can see this at three levels: (i) When we think about our own lives, the gradually growing awareness that we have only so much time left enhances our love of life and our resolve to make the best use we can of what remains to us. So precious does life gradually become to us that we can be acutely aware of loving it even at times when we are very ill. (ii) When we look at ephemeral things in nature, such as my beloved insects, we are deeply touched by their unquestioning affirmation of their own brief lives, their busyness, their battling to do what they have got to do. (iii) Hardest of all, and most rarely discussed, is the question of how we are to accept the mortality of those who are dearest of all to us. But it has always been said that marriage is 'till death us do part'. And it is this realization, that every human love gets its peculiar depth and its poignancy from the knowledge of mortality that always qualifies it, that makes what I call 'solar marriage' possible.

Transient oneself, to say an unconditional Yes to transience; and mortal oneself, to love a fellow mortal — that is the best there is for us humans. Any other doctrine is a lie.

Doing without stars

From Homer to Hollywood, the entire First Axial Period was characterized by a tendency to the hero worship or idolization of the 'star' human being. The desire to be a follower or a fan has been equally strong in secular and religious contexts: the charismatic or exceptional figure, in the past usually but not quite always male, is a leader, an example, a teacher, a messiah, or someone of extraordinary artistic powers: he is the hero, the national deliverer, the saint, the guru, the lawgiver, the creative artist, the genius, the saviour, and — most recently — the star.

The star is a very democratized figure. He hardly needs any special abilities except 'star quality' and the ability to project it, for example by film acting. The star is the person everyone wants to be, and has been the first category of celebrity to be equally open to both sexes.

The star, as the word implies, is a human being who has something heavenly about her: she is a highly 'public' figure, who shines and radiates 'glory'. She is described as queenly, or as a diva or goddess. A human being like this, whose fame is going to live on, and who attracts religious awe, appeared relatively infrequently at the beginning of the First Axial Period but today is commonplace. In any large developed country there must be up to about five hundred of them at any one time.

Inevitably, the star tends to be seen as a demigod and therefore as an immortal — even if nowadays she is immortal only in recordings and computer simulations. In earlier times the exceptional human being might even ascend to heaven and perhaps return therefrom in an hour of great need. He was credited with a number of

divine powers: he might work miracles, and create truth. He could
be seen as a cosmic Lord like Jesus or the Buddha. He was so great
and inspiring that lesser mortals took pride in the mere fact that he
had once lived on earth amongst them: thus when Einstein died a
newspaper cartoon showed the earth as seen from outer space, with a
big notice planted in it reading: ALBERT EINSTEIN LIVED HERE.

This cult of personality – as we have noted already – was linked
with a more general spiritual individualism that was characteristic of
the entire First Axial Period. There was a strong desire to believe in
the uniqueness of each individual person, a doctrine reflected in the
common custom of taking a new name 'in religion' when one under-
went some rite of passage. Each angel or spirit was a distinct species,
and each human rational soul had a unique destiny and a unique
relation to God. In this context one might see the cult of the saint or
the genius – the person whose individuality is so vivid and so fully
developed and expressed that her name will never die – as making it
a little easier for us lesser mortals to believe that we too might be
capable of personal salvation and immortality.

Admiration for the genius and belief in his extraordinary status
has been as common amongst the great philosophers as it has been
amongst ordinary people. Kierkegaard makes sarcastic jokes about
Hegel's propensity to confuse himself with the Absolute; but
Kierkegaard describes *himself* as a genius, and in any case Hegel's tendency to confuse himself with God is eclipsed by that of Descartes.
For to an extraordinary degree Descartes' philosophy pictures the single rational individual as a self-founding subject who can rebuild all
reality from scratch in thought and know it (in principle) as thoroughly and transparently as God himself knows it. One cannot imagine that any claim for the status of the individual was ever pitched
higher than that – even though it is conventional to suggest that
some of the German Idealists (Fichte, Max Stirner) went even higher.

Such an inflated cult of the individual was bound to crash as
people began to understand the implications of two lines of thought:
the first points out that language precedes thought, and language is
through and through a public creation and public property.
Individual thought is therefore always secondary, and there can be
no such isolated and self-founding human subject as Descartes pre-
tended to be. Therefore philosophers need nowadays to listen to language, exactly as political leaders need nowadays to listen to public

106

opinion. And the second line of argument says that it is a mistake to suppose that history is created entirely by the actions of great men. On the contrary, in our modern large scale mass societies we have become aware of the way that deep change in the human world is brought about by a sea change in the communally generated consensus: the climate of thought, public opinion, the fashion, the state of the argument, the deep assumptions of a particular historical period, and so on. The work of a talented individual may crystallize a change that is already taking place, but before that, general cultural conditions have to be such as can produce such an individual and afford him a hearing. In the end, it is more true that history makes great men than that great men make history.

During the nineteenth century the whole issue was debated between two parties, the Prophets and the Democrats. The Prophets (Carlyle, Emerson, Nietzsche, and others) still looked to the great man, the genius, to renew culture and save the world. Nietzsche, indeed, was rather puzzling, in that he *both* led the attack on the self *and* proclaimed the Over-man.

The other party, the Democrats (including socialists and anarchists) give priority to social history and to ordinary language. (Some figures who ought to have been more consistent Democrats were distracted by worries about whether they themselves were or were not geniuses: Wittgenstein is an example.[1]) In the late twentieth century it became apparent that old style individual genius had dried up: it had in any case usually flourished amongst the relatively very small élites in city states such as those of ancient Athens, and pre-unification Italy and Germany. Late modern societies are relatively abounding with high levels of specialization, both of knowledge and of technologies. Under these new conditions, brilliant managers of large scale projects replace the geniuses of the past, and we all of us become aware of the extent to which we are creatures of our own times. We no longer live hooked into God, or into our own 'White Goddess': we live hooked into the mass media, from which we all absorb a great deal each day.*

---

*'The White Goddess' was Robert Graves's term for his Muse. Picasso was perhaps the culminating and final example of the genius who lives for and by nothing else but his own talent, which (so Picasso thought) gave him magical or even godlike powers. Today, by contrast, the most highly gifted people are and have to be team players, whose joint productions are very much period pieces.

It is hard to exaggerate the extent to which we are creatures of fashion and are continually being changed by and with the times. But to take a very simple example, just consider how the shape of a car can change from being disconcertingly novel to being comfortable within two years and to looking a bit tired and out of date within seven. The culture within which we live continuously alters our very perceptions; and in the same way it changes our moral responses too. I don't need to recall the painful story of the extent to which men of my own generation have been morally reconstructed by cultural changes since the 1950s; but I can console myself by pointing out that my contemporaries who have denounced relativism, resisted reconstruction, and tried to remain unchanged have all ended up as preposterous old dinosaurs.

All this goes to show that the old idea of a metaphysical self, an immortal finite spiritual substance, is dead. The self is radically linguistic and historical. And with the concept of the soul dies also the belief in the saint or the genius, if by these terms we mean people who have personal qualities that somehow transcend time and change. Nobody does: is it not obvious that medieval saints were just medieval people, only more so; and that most of the geniuses of more recent centuries were just hard working and ambitious intellectuals who were lucky because they happened to catch the tide and say just what their age was ready to hear someone say?

And hence too the democratic form of this book. It doesn't profess to give you The Answer. It says that we should give up all forms of the idea that somebody, somewhere, knows The Answer. That's a silly idea, rather like the idea in an old-fashioned thriller that the fate of the world depends upon the fate of a scientist who alone knows a magic formula. Instead, we should learn the peculiar joys of religious thinking for ourselves; and we should also listen to our own times and pay attention to the way the consensus is currently shifting.

Chapter Seventeen

Nothing Is Hidden

Bertrand Russell once complained that everyone seemed to assume that it would be a good thing for us all to hold more, and more definite, beliefs. 'Whereas it seems to me', he said, 'that we'd all be better off if we believed a lot *less*.'

I'd put the point more strongly: progress in our thinking consists very largely in coming to recognize how much we have been guided, and indeed dominated, by false assumptions. One by one to recognize these assumptions, expose them, question them, and get rid of them is a great liberation. It clears one's head.

Above all, this is true of the Big Question, the one that people pose about the Meaning of Life. People reckon that the Big Question is the one that philosophy ought to help us to answer and that religion purports to guard the truth about, truth which it has received by revelation. The Question is stated with great urgency, as if people are quite sure that it is a real question and a very big one; but the wording is varied and more than a little vague. It runs thus: Why are we here? What's it all in aid of? What is the meaning of life? What's it all supposed to be about? Can *you* see any purpose behind it all? What were we put on this earth for? And so on.

Now when a psychologist hears a puzzled and distressed person complain and fire off questions like these, she plays them back with a straight bat by saying: 'What makes you want to ask that? How do you feel about that?' A philosopher similarly can play it straight down the middle by replying: 'What are you asking for? Who do you think might know the answer to that one? Do you think you'll be able to recognize the correct answer if you come across it?'

So imagine that a philosopher questions the ordinary person to find out what prompts the question, and what might be acceptable as an answer to it. I think you'll agree that the ordinary person's Big Question springs from the assumption that we've a right to know what's going on. The world has a duty to make sense to us. But what we find is that the world and our life in it is a chronic puzzle. There's something that we are not being told. We are in the situation of servants who are receiving and carrying out orders but whose master and mistress are not taking us fully into their confidence. There *is* a full story, but we haven't yet been *told* the full story and are fretting as a result. When we know the Full Story, we'll be content. Everything will make sense to us.

We already have an astonishingly large and complex set of assumptions here, but there's more yet. As they approach death, the Big Question becomes more urgent for people. From what they have said to me, I have gathered that they think that if there is a life after death, we may expect to find in and through death the Answer that we seek. In a word, people expect truth in death but only if there is indeed a life after death. So they ask me what I think about life after death. In a word: 'Can I expect soon to know, at last, what it has all been about?' They seek reassurance.

In the parts of the social world that I know best, at least 90% of people think in these terms: that is, they are seriously troubled by a version of the Big Question that rests on this complex body of assumptions. No doubt they'd call themselves 'agnostics', on the grounds that they don't know the Answer to the Big Question. But their assumptions, that there *is* a Big Question, that it does make sense, and there is or should be an Answer to it somewhere to be found, presuppose a highly complex world view about which they seem not to be agnostic at all. That is clearly paradoxical – and, of course, I'm in a very paradoxical position myself, for I'm saying that (round here, at least, where ordinary people such as academics are gathered together) well over 90% of people are in a bad muddle and need to clear their heads of a great mass of long out-of-date ideas. I profess to be democratic – but I now seem to be saying that the democratic age cannot really begin until ordinary people give up their ancient assumptions and illusions.

For, consider: the most important of these assumptions is the assumption that our life is a riddle to us. Something's hidden, and why? We need to go back to the old polytheistic world view and to the decidedly archaic idea that the gods are a bit jealous and scornful of us. They think we are getting a bit too big for our boots, and in order to keep us in our place they are withholding information from us. They muck us about a bit: they mock us, they give us apparently arbitrary orders and don't explain why. They are obliging us to bite our lips, keep quiet, and keep our heads down. All will be made clear eventually.

The ordinary person's Big Question about the point of it all has some other ancient elements in it as well. The most important is platonism: the surface phenomena of life are not very clearly rational, but there is a hidden Intelligible Order in which everything makes perfect sense. The intelligible world is also the eternal world towards which we journey and which we will enter in death – that is why death is the way to truth. So life does have a hidden meaning, and philosophers are trained to work their way through to it – and there is more than that, for not only is there a ready-made Intelligible Order out there waiting for us to find it, but also there is a ready-made or pre-established fit between our minds and the objective rational order of things. So not only is there a big Answer waiting out there ready-made for us, but also *we* are ready-made to be able to understand it. In this life we are exiled from our true home in the eternal world, but never mind, we will all of us go home soon.

There is one last Big Assumption to be pointed out. It comes chiefly from Christian theology. It is the assumption that the Whole Story is some form of Grand Narrative of cosmic fall and redemption, a story in which each of us has a part to play that is already scripted for him. When we understand the Whole Story we will see that the various evils and mysteries that formerly bothered us so much now turn out to be justified in view of the way the whole drama is going. In the end, It All makes sense.

Such are the main assumptions underlying ordinary people's questions about the Meaning of Life and the Point of It All. What are we to do about all these assumptions? In *The Hitch-Hiker's Guide to the Galaxy* the comic writer Douglas Adams simply ridicules the Big Question about the Meaning of Life, the Universe, and Everything, and his huge and entirely justified popularity shows that

111

the same ordinary people who ask the Big Question in such an anguished way are also capable of recognizing that it *is* a silly question and they should not have asked it. (I have to seize upon that point to justify my own claim to be a democratic philosopher of religion who wants to encourage ordinary people to think for themselves and trust their own judgement. I am right, provided that I remind the same ordinary people that they are wisest when they are most resolutely mocking and sceptical.)

I conclude that ordinary people's Big Questions about life after death, the meaning of life, and the point of it all rest upon a large body of wildly obsolete assumptions about the way the Universe has to be. Bring the assumptions out into the open, see how absurd they are, abandon them – and a great burden falls from our shoulders. Wittgenstein saw all this very clearly. He simply refused to take the Big Question seriously, saying that everything lies open to view, nothing is hidden, and there is therefore nothing to explain. I agree. There is no mystery. Our life is not a preparation. We are not going anywhere special. The world is ours: we are at home already.

People sometimes snap at me for saying that there is no mystery. But I can reply: Exactly what reason do you have for allowing your life to be dominated by the assumption that our life is a mystery, and that the Answer to it all is hidden somewhere behind the scenes, ready to be found if we will but look hard enough in the right place? What reason do we have for assuming all this? And the answer is, none at all.

When we give up the idea that our chief religious task is to discover and hold on to some very important but hidden Truth and when we thus get our heads clear, *then* we'll be ready to see that our chief religious task is to love this world and this life and to make the most of them that we possibly can. So far as I can see, no other option presents itself any longer.

Chapter Eighteen

Warnings

So a new Plato, a new Buddha? Certainly not. I have been suggesting that the First Axial Age, usually dated from 800 to 200 B.C.E., was an age of great founding teachers, each of whom attracted a mass following and became the source of a major and long lasting cultural tradition in the Middle East, in India, or in China. But, we said, the Second Axial Age will be different. The 'genius' and the teacher-disciple relationship are out of date. What we will want to see is the thoroughgoing democratization both of religion and of thought generally. To that end, we don't need another orthodoxy: we need a teaching that will show how the ordinary individual can learn to think and live creatively and so experience religious joy in life.

The Second Axial Age is not an age when most people are peasants with only very limited access to education and culture. It is an intensely communicative period, in which almost everyone is going to be highly aware of being a part of the whole – i.e., connected into, and playing a part in, the entire communicative life of humankind. We are not missing anything: on the contrary, we are connected up with everything. So we don't need a mediator to link the individual with the whole. Rather, we need to learn to make the best use of the amazing cultural resources that are now available to each of us, so that we can all play our full part in the life of the whole – the point here being that to achieve life satisfaction a person needs not just *individual* self-realization but also the consciousness of having made some contribution to the common life of the *whole*.

It is also a characteristic of the new period that — to repeat a phrase — 'nothing is hidden'. We give up the idea of elite knowledge, into which an elite few have been initiated. This idea, prominent in Plato's *Republic*, has had a long history: the elite may be a group of highly trained philosopher-kings; they may be a group of monks who have become personally proficient in the way to salvation; they may be a group of high priests who are the accredited custodians and interpreters of revealed and saving truth; or they may be an academic elite such as the professoriate in general or the professional scientists in particular, who guard and approve each addition to the body of knowledge on which the well-being of society as a whole depends. We need to break with this tradition, and I have been trying to do so by insisting that there are no mysteries and there is no hidden truth; for on the contrary, the way to truth and happiness in philosophy and religion is broad and easy. All we need is to throw off the inhibitions and the 'blocking ideas' that are the legacy of our past. When we do that, when we have fully cleared our heads, then truth is easy. It is before our very eyes. I believe that the quickest way to it is simply by grasping the ideas of Emptiness and brightness.

At this point, however, it is necessary to repeat a caveat. I have been suggesting an analogy: fully democratized and spontaneously lived Second Axial Age religion is to the traditional, mediated, institutional kind of religion with which everyone is familiar very much as jazz is to traditional European 'classical' music. Jazz is music that has become post-historical, extempore, readily collaborative: art off the cuff. It sounds easy — but of course it calls for very considerable talent and training, and could perhaps have been invented only by an oppressed and culturally deprived people whose history had largely de-traditionalized them. We would be deceiving ourselves if we were to suppose that we could instantly shrug off our long training in European music and become as spontaneously creative as the great jazz musicians were.

Similarly, I suggest that in order to get to the point at which we can become spontaneously creative religious thinkers and actors, we must first lose everything and have experienced the Void. Before one can make a really fresh start, one must become poor in spirit, one must have entered nihilism, one must have lost one's past self, one must have lost everything. And, to be less rhetorical and more specific, this means above all that we must rid ourselves of all the platonic assumptions with which people still instinctively approach philosophical and (especially) religious questions. For example, people see religion as a way to gain some vital but presently hidden knowledge that brings happiness and will change their lives. This belief in ready-made enlightenment is harmful, because it makes people easy prey for gurus. Keep saying to yourself: 'There is no ready-made saving truth, and there is no person specially authorized to allow me access to it.'

Furthermore, to a remarkable extent New Religious Movements and alternative therapies still set about trying to construct a parallel 'spiritual world' or 'dimension' alongside the world of everyday life, and invoke 'spiritual' powers, 'energies' and 'forces' unknown to science. They often borrow some of the vocabulary of science, but the claims made *never ever* reach scientific standards of clarity and testability. It is striking that during the twentieth century NRMs largely disclaimed theism and gave up producing their own scriptures; but almost all of them still cling to a remnant of platonism – and by doing so have become an intellectual mess. In reply, one can do no better than to quote the admirable title of a Quaker pamphlet: 'There is Another World But it is This One',[1] and stick strictly to scientific method, the senses, ordinary language, and this life. The Purgative Way – getting rid of all the errors and false assumptions with which our heads are clogged – leads in the end to a condition of utter Emptiness in which we at last become ready to see the easiness and obviousness of a religious re-vision-ing of this world and this life.

Make a friend of the Void. This is a difficult point to make because people in the 'Western' group of cultures – Jewish, Christian, and Islamic – have been so strongly indoctrinated to be terrified of the Void and to use their faith as a defence against it. All that we have in our tradition to recommend the Void to us is the traditional mystic's 'divine nothingness' – in Kabbalah, the En Sof, the Godhead *in nihilo suo absconditus* (hidden in its own nothingness); and in Christian platonism, God's transcendence of *all* the categories of our thinking, so that Gregory of Nyssa can equate 'creation out of nothing' with 'creation out of God'.[2] To these familiar but philosophically obscure mystical ideas can be added the traditional symbolism of night and darkness, vigil and waiting, the dead Christ, Holy Saturday, and Tenebrae. These ideas have familiarized us in the West with the idea of waiting in deep darkness for dawn and rebirth – but the sting has been withdrawn, because while we are in church on Holy Saturday thinking about the despair of Jesus' followers as his corpse lies in the tomb, we all know that the dawn will come. The whole setting in which we wait is friendly, supernaturalist, reassuring. *Of course* we know that dawn will come. But I'm thinking of a much more complete loss than that. I'm thinking of the condition of Samuel Beckett's characters, or of Paul Celan. I'm thinking about how I will react on the day when I learn that my own illness is terminal. (Wittgenstein did not complain. He said simply, 'Good', and went on working.)

Make a friend of the Void. Practise by meditation and (if it helps) by seeking out the bleakest, emptiest landscapes. And above all, do not be led astray by your own desire for 'meaning'. People's religious hunger is very great, and it all too often takes the form of a desire for 'meaning' – a very obscure notion, but it always seems to involve a nostalgic harking back to just the kind of religion that we can't have any more: a ready-made intelligibility of the world, ready-made truth, good omens, and signs everywhere of a welcoming, built-in purposiveness in the way things go which indicates that our presence in the world is pre-planned and we are being watched over. Our anxious expectation of such things is so strong that we are too easily persuaded that we have found them. It has often been pointed out that many religious systems incorporate carefully designed 'blocks to falsifiability', and when such a system meets our own eager desire to be deceived, we can very easily fall victim to it. The best protection is a strictly naturalistic and sceptical outlook and a determination not to locate religious meaning and value anywhere else but in this world, in this life, and in the here and now.

Conclusions

According to the current popular convention, the future will belong entirely to technology. Human beings will have neither the leisure nor the inclination to think: they will be nothing but the operators of (usually rather violent) machines. A dismal prospect, but if there do continue to be people who feel an urgent need to understand the human condition and who ask themselves how they should live, then we have tried to describe a new world-view and ethic that may come to prevail amongst them. I am not suggesting that it has been wholly created by any individual thinker, but that it represents an already emergent consensus. We may come to see the present time as part of a Second Axial Age and the new world view and ethic as opening up a Second Axial Period.

The new world view and ethic may seem very queer and novel to readers new to this field, but we have already explored its leading themes from enough angles to have gained some idea of how they work. I hope that you will know how to understand the sentences if I summarize the world view as follows:

Everything is contingent; that is, everything is happenstance. If something happens according to a rule, well then, it just *happens* to happen according to a rule; and because our account of what the rules are is always subject to modification, we do not attempt to ground the rules in any postulated unchanging order behind the scenes. There is only all this, the apparent world, the human life-world. *Our* world is *the* world, the only world. *We* have given it order, and *we* formulate and revise all the rules.

The world of life is beginningless, endless, outsideless, and in ceaseless change. It is all there is. It has three aspects or modes: Be-ing, Language, and Brightness. By Be-ing we mean the dance of possibility in the Void, the ceaseless gentle forthcomingness of finite existence in time. By Language we mean the endless to and fro of human symbolic exchange. It is within the flux of our human communication that Be-ing is formed into beings, and the common human life world is produced and held steady. As we think in language, so we always see the world in terms of our language: hence we can always *tell* what we see. Within the flux of our communication everything else is produced, too, as any library will show you: linguistic meaning, knowledge, values, art, religion — and because language is so reflexive, general and allusive, its motion also produces Brightness, by which I mean the world's vividness and beauty in our (and *only* our) conscious awareness of it. Everything might have been dark, unknowing and quite unaware, but the world in fact becomes bright and beautiful in our awareness of it. We complete the world. It's ours.

We called this world view 'Empty radical humanism' because we recognize that we ourselves are just as much mere transient products of the motion of language as everything else is; but we are the only speakers, the only batters-back-and-forth of language, and in us alone it all comes together, makes sense, adds up to a whole, and becomes worthwhile. Thus our existence is justified.

With this world view we associate a religion of life that is ardently committed to life in its very transience, loves the world's Brightness as other humans once loved the divine Glory, and is committed to the fellow human simply as such. In our social ethics, we are concerned *only* with attempting to free our fellow humans from need or relative deprivation. We prefer to leave the work of *governing* human beings to the law, and to the processes of liberal democratic politics. Moralism has a very bad record, and we should surely prefer to follow the minimalist approach of liberal democracy to questions of personal ethics: the presumption should always be in favour of toleration, and the freedom of others should be limited only where it is demonstrably (and enforceably) necessary to limit it for the good of others.

Such, in briefest sketch, is the emergent world-view, religion and ethics of a Second Axial Age. You may think it very odd: why does it differ so much from the world-view of the First Axial period, with which many people are still content?

The crux is no doubt the anti-realist view of the objective world, which still shocks many people. The old doctrine of Creation has always suggested that we have a fully formed and ready-made world specially designed for us, which was all finished and prepared for the first human beings before ever they appeared on Earth. Against this background, the human contribution to the world tends even to this day to be seen in starkly negative terms: Nature is pure and virginal, until we come along and pollute, contaminate or spoil her. As the early nineteenth century hymn has it: 'Every prospect pleases / And only man is vile'. But I have been calling for the overthrow of that picture. The only complete world that has ever been seen is a world seen by human eyes, a world that human language and human theorizing have already differentiated, described, theorized and, above all, *appropriated*. The only world we have ever seen is one that we have already made our own, and so far as we are concerned our world is the only world there is. Thus science does not copy a pre-existent and fully formed divinely ordered cosmos in which all things are already bright and beautiful; no, science starts from the human everyday life world and further differentiates, theorizes, and enriches it, making it vastly larger and more complex than it was in the past. In the process, we find the world becoming completely appropriated to us; but we *also* find ourselves becoming completely appropriated to our world.

This double process has helped to restore an ancient continuity. In Bronze Age times, the gods, humans, animals, sky, earth, and underworld were all parts of one continuous whole. Then in the Axial Age Greeks invented the ideas of rational enquiry, Nature, a natural order, a systematic programme of research, the application of mathematics to nature, and an organized body of knowledge. The invention of Nature as a relatively autonomous realm had far-reaching consequences. The gods withdrew to a supernatural world, and the desacralization of nature began. Humans began to take a pessimistic view of this world, this life, and the body, and to look for the possibility of gaining otherworldly salvation in the heavenly world after death. The body/soul distinction was invented, with the idea that the soul would master the body and eventually be delivered from it. The First Axial Period thus developed a curious dual ambition to 'conquer' Nature. In religion one sought by asceticism to conquer nature in oneself and to purify oneself in the hope of gaining eternal happiness in the supernatural world; while in science and technology one sought a complete and godlike knowledge of the world in order to wield something like divine mastery over it. Thus in the First Axial Period there was a certain analogy between the believer's attitude to his own body and the scientist's attitude to Nature. It was a dualistic period and a period in which there was a certain mutual sympathy between monotheistic religion and natural science.

Nobody, I think, foresaw what was eventually to happen. Descartes established Early Modern science as the mathematical analysis of the workings of the world machine by a spirit intelligence that was independent of it. But as the development of science proceeded, it more and more incorporated first the human body and then the whole human being into its subject matter. Especially since Darwin, philosophers have seen thought becoming more and more immanentist. We no longer see the movement of things as being ordered from outside, but as self-ordering. Living organisms, language, consciousness, culture, systems of knowledge – all these things increasingly look as if they give birth to themselves and order themselves purely immanently. That is why the breathtaking growth of knowledge nowadays has rendered all traditional and metaphysical world views obsolete.

That in turn is why we are seeing Second Axial Period thinking as dominated by the themes of communication and a constantly shifting, always emergent consensus. It tends to see meaning as current use, truth as the current state of the argument, and reality as never more than provisionally constructed within an endless open conversation. We must now leave behind us a world in which the mind found rest in contemplating eternal reality and embrace instead a world of endless exchange and change. We need to learn to love transience, because it's all there is, and we are part of it. Heraclitus has turned out to have been right: everything flows. I'm not complaining at all, because I already find, and I think you find, that the new, man-made and ever-changing world is just as beautiful as the old one ever was. More beautiful, in fact: mortal ourselves, we can learn a divine love for everything else that is just as mortal as we are.

Notes

Notes in a book always involve the text in appeal to standard authorities within an established tradition and are therefore somewhat out of place here, when we should be trying to avoid appealing to any particular readership or to any established tradition. But of course nobody really starts from nowhere, so I have persuaded myself to include a very few notes and references.

Introduction
1. My terminology here is of course borrowed from Thomas S. Kuhn, *The Structure of Scientific Revolutions.*

Chapter 1
1. The ideas in this section were first put forward in my *After God, The Religion of Being,* and *The Revelation of Being.*

Chapter 3
1. Stephen Batchelor, *Verses from the Center,* p. 116.
2. Jay L. Garfield, *Fundamental Wisdom,* p. 253.

Chapter 5
1. Cupitt, *The New Religion of Life.*

Chapter 6
1. Cupitt, *After All,* p.109.

Chapter 7
1. On this theme, see C.W. Huntington Jr., *The Emptiness of Emptiness.*
2. L. Kolakowski, *Metaphysical Horror.*
3. La Source (1856), in the Louvre, Paris.

Chapter 8
1. Nietzsche, *The Will to Power,* p. 3.
2. Nietzsche, *The Will to Power,* p. 7.
3. De Selincourt edition, p. 30.
4. Cited in the De Selincourt edition, p. 255, in the endnote on the lines quoted in the text, above.

Chapter 12
    1. Conveniently available in David Farrell Krell (ed.), *Martin Heidegger*. The phrases quoted are to be found on pp. 432f.
    2. See Cupitt, *The New Religion of Life*.

Chapter 14
    1. The account that follows differs somewhat from that which was given in Cupitt, *The Revelation of Being*.
    2. From the 'later writings', twelve chapters appended to the Shobo-genzo, no.4, translated in Yuho Yokoi, *Zen Master Dogen*, p. 108

Chapter 16
    1. David Avraham Weiner, *Genius and Talent*.

Chapter 18
    1. Jean Hardy, 'There is Another World But it is This One'.
    2. R. J. Zwi Werblowsky, 'God as Nothing', pp. 39f.

Bibliography

Batchelor, Stephen. *Verses from the Center: A Buddhist Vision of the Sublime.* New York: Riverhead books, Penguin Putnam, 2000.

Cupitt, Don. *After All: Religion without Alienation.* London: SCM Press, 1994.

_____. *After God.* New York: Basic Books 1997.

_____. *The New Religion of Life in Everyday Speech.* London: SCM Press, 1999.

_____. *The Religion of Being.* London: SCM Press, 1998.

_____. *The Revelation of Being.* London: SCM Press, 1998.

Krell, David Farrell, ed. *Martin Heidegger: Basic Writings.* London: Routledge, 1993.

Garfield, Jay L. *The Fundamental Wisdom of the Middle Way: Nagarjuna's Mulamadhyamakakarika.* New York: Oxford University Press, 1995.

Hardy, Jean. 'There is Another World But it is This One', London: Quaker Universalist Group pamphlet no.12, 1988.

Huntington Jr., C.W. *The Emptiness of Emptiness: An Introduction to Early Indian Madhyamika.* Honolulu: University of Hawaii Press, 1989.

Kolakowski, L. *Metaphysical Horror.* Oxford: Blackwell, 1988.

Kuhn, Thomas S. *The Structure of Scientific Revolutions.* The University of Chicago Press, 1962.

Nietzsche, Friedrich. *The Will to Power*, tr. Walter Kaufmann. New York: Vintage Books, 1968.

de Selincourt, Ernest, ed. *Wordsworth: The Prelude, or Growth of a Poet's Mind (Text of 1805).* Oxford and New York: The Oxford University Press, 1970.

Velmans, Max. *Understanding Consciousness.* London: Routledge, 2000.

Weiner, David Avraham. *Genius and Talent: Schopenhauer's Influence on Wittgenstein's Early Philosophy.* London: Associated University Presses, 1992.

Werblowsky, R.J. Zwi. 'God as Nothing in the Kabbalah'; in Robert E. Carter (ed.), *God, the Self and Nothingness: Reflections Eastern and Western.* New York: Paragon House, 1990, pp.37–43.

Yokoi, Yuho. *Zen Master Dogen.* (New York: Weatherhill, 1976.

Index